Doing Your Child Obs Case Study

A Step-by-Step Guide

Doing Your Child Observation Case Study

A Step-by-Step Guide

Cath Arnold

Open University Press

Open University Press
McGraw-Hill Education
McGraw-Hill House
Shoppenhangers Road
Maidenhead
Berkshire
England
SL6 2QL

email: enquiries@openup.co.uk
world wide web: www.openup.co.uk

and Two Penn Plaza, New York, NY 10121-2289, USA

First published 2015

A catalogue record of this book is available from the British Library

ISBN-13: 978-0-335-26372-1
ISBN-10: 0-335-26372-0
eISBN: 978-0-335-26373-8

Library of Congress Cataloging-in-Publication Data
CIP data applied for

Typeset by Transforma Pvt. Ltd., Chennai, India

Printed and bound by CPI Group (UK) Ltd, Croydon, CR0 4YY

Praise for this book

"This is a fascinating and accessible new book on child observation case study for students and professionals. Cath Arnold integrates theoretical perspectives and practical examples of observations with remarkable clarity in this comprehensive guidance to child case study."
Shirley Allen, Senior Lecturer Early Childhood Studies, Middlesex University

"It is quickly evident to the reader that 'Doing Your Child Observation Case Study' is steeped in the expertise and extensive experience of its author. The practical guidance it offers is likely to prove invaluable for childhood studies students and early career researchers in the field. Yet Cath Arnold's 'step-by-step guide' goes far beyond the practical. She shines vital light on the complex nuances of values, beliefs, ethics and rights inherent in child case study and addresses with clarity and credibility the crucial role that theory can play in supporting our understanding of children's actions. This text is an excellent addition to the childhood studies bookshelf."
Dr Jane Murray, Centre for Education and Research,
University of Northampton, UK

"Cath Arnold has provided a rich resource for those who want to understand more about children, their wellbeing and their learning. This detailed approach to child observation offers guidance on why, how and what to observe, and how to interpret what is observed. Rich in examples collected over many years 'Doing your Child Observation Case Study' will get many early years practitioners started on their own learning journeys as they watch and engage with young children to develop detailed impressions of children's development."
Professor Cathy Nutbrown, Head of The School of Education,
The University of Sheffield

"In this new book Cath is once more supporting early childhood educators to engage in the strong UK tradition of child observations; the tradition of Piaget, Novara, Darwin and Susan Isaacs. She has developed her own understanding of the importance of observational studies building on the giants whose shoulders we all stand on. This powerful publication combines insights into both the theory and practice of developing child observations in an early years setting. Cath demonstrates how detailed and powerful records of children's learning and development speak to practitioners and hold their value over time in a world where early educators are increasingly obliged to devote enormous amounts of their energy filling in forms, schedules and are hard pressed to reject the pressure of tick box developmental checks and imposed tracking schemes.

This book lights the way to a much deeper way of documenting children's learning and development. As educators we need to match children's learning with rich curriculum content and this book reminds us that we can only achieve this critical pedagogical task if we have closely watched what it is that excites and interests each individual child. 'Doing Your Child Observation Case Study' shows us the way to be well informed practitioners able to offer children a really rich learning experience."
Dr Margy Whalley, Director of the Research, Development and Training Base
at the Pen Green Centre and Centre for Children and their Families

Dedication

I would like to dedicate this book to my five grandchildren: Georgia, Harry, Nicole, Gabriella and Anya. A special mention goes to Georgia, who has been involved (as an adult now) in selecting material about her early childhood to be included in this volume.

Contents

List of figures and tables

Figures

Tables

Introduction

Alex (aged 3): 'Do you know Martin?'

Me: 'No, I don't know Martin'

Alex: 'Say Martin'

Me: 'Martin'

Alex: 'You know Martin now'

(Mairs and the Pen Green Team, ed. Arnold, 2012: 170)

Every interaction we, as adults, have with a child, offers the potential for us to gain some insight into that child's thinking. For example, this short conversation I had with a little boy called Alex intrigued me because it tells me so much about his current understanding of 'knowing people' or 'knowing about people'. Even if Martin had been present and Alex had introduced me to him, I still would not have felt that I 'knew' him. It is these little nuances in our 'knowing' that have fascinated me for the past 25 years or more.

This book offers a step-by-step guide to studying children and constructing a child observation case study. It draws on a particular philosophical approach, which is described in Chapter 1. The book also draws on a long history of studying children that dates back to at least the eighteenth century. We have been able to gain deep insights from studies that parents such as Charles Darwin and Jean Piaget have offered, as well as educators like Frederick Froebel, Susan Isaacs and Caroline Pratt. In addition, and from a medical and psychological perspective, we can also draw on the work of Freud and Winnicott. All of these researchers used child observation as a method to come up with theories about children's growth and development.

Given the history, it is quite difficult, as a novice, to know where to start. It is my firm belief that starting with children and with observing children is essential, so there will be some guidance and examples in this book of what those observations might look like.

Georgia

Following in the footsteps of many renowned writers and researchers, I focused on observing Georgia, my eldest granddaughter, in order to construct a child observation case study – first, for my master's thesis and subsequently in my first book, *Child Development and Learning 2–5 years: Georgia's Story* (Arnold, 1999). Georgia was systematically observed, as a young child, at home, by her parents and grandparents, and, at nursery, by her nursery workers. The data was analysed in relation to the AIRSS framework – autonomy, involvement, relationships, schemas and strategies (Arnold, 1997) – a framework I developed when studying Georgia and three other children for my master's degree in Education, and by considering the traditional subject areas of writing and reading, understanding mathematical concepts, developing scientific concepts and emotional development (Arnold, 1999). I will be using the process of studying Georgia and some of the original data gathered throughout this book. I want to emphasise that I am not providing a perfect 'model' to follow but that much can be learned through seeing different examples. Sharing observations of one child, Georgia, throughout the book offers some sort of continuity.

The purpose of doing a child study

It is helpful, at the outset, to think about the 'purpose' of carrying out a child study. First, is it a requirement for a course being undertaken? Even if you are required to carry out a child study, you need to be thinking about what you hope to learn. Is it purely to understand that child better? Or is it to be able to provide for that child's learning more effectively? Or is it to identify that child's learning retrospectively? How can the knowledge we gain from studying one child transfer to other children? A parent recently asked me, 'What is the point of identifying a child's schemas?' and I really had to think about this question. I think it is about identifying what each child is motivated to learn about and capitalising on that motivation. I like to try to stay very close to what a child is trying to learn about when offering further experiences. I do not always succeed, but I do try.

Identifying your principles and values

Whether you are a parent, early childhood educator or a student, your approach will undoubtedly be underpinned by your principles and values. So it is definitely worth reflecting on what you believe in, as far as raising and educating children is concerned. If you are part of a team of carers for one child or in a nursery or other early childhood setting, where you are responsible for the care and education of a group or groups of children, reflecting on your beliefs together will help make those beliefs explicit. There will, of course, be small differences. If the differences are too great, then it will be quite difficult to work together.

An exercise to identify values and beliefs

Complete the following sentence stems as individuals, then discuss in pairs and, finally, as a team.

- The best thing about working with young children is …
- Working with young children can be a challenge when …
- I like interacting with parents when …
- I feel intimidated by parents when …
- I chose this profession because …

An example of a set of beliefs that went unchallenged for some time (in a private nursery I managed for three years).

A simple example is whether you allow children to climb up the slide or walk down the slide when they are able. I can remember the days when what resounded from every playground or nursery was quite a loud 'Come down properly! On your bottom!' It was a rule no one seemed to question, until …

One day we asked ourselves what children were learning from climbing up the slide or from walking down the slide. We realised that children were learning through their own bodies, by using them in different ways, about slopes and 'angles'. What could be more important than mathematical knowledge? We also realised that they did not attempt these feats until they were 'masters' of 'coming down properly on their bottoms'. So we asked ourselves whether we want children to challenge themselves and of course, we do.

Staying 'open' to what children are showing an interest in

Child study requires an openness to what children are showing us about themselves and their learning. If we jump in with 'What colour is it?' or 'How many are there?' at every opportunity, the chances are that we will cut across their learning. So, at the least, trying to be unobtrusive and certainly trying not to dominate the situation, helps. Some observation methods are more subtle than others. Fortunately the days of huge video cameras are long gone, however even if we are using much smaller devices, we still need each child's permission, on every occasion. Ethics is a huge issue that is hotly debated, and Chapter 2 is dedicated to exploring some of the issues. Chapter 3 looks at the different techniques and tools you can use.

Gathering observations without making initial judgements takes some skill and practice. In fact, we all make judgements about what we are seeing all of the time, but it helps to be aware of the kinds of judgements you are making. Sharing your observations with a friend, relative or colleague can help you to see things from a different perspective. If you are working in a setting, sharing your observations of their child with the parents or carers is essential. They are much more likely to be able to provide you with more information and a more accurate reading of their child's intentions. You, in turn, can share ideas about the curriculum your setting is using, with them.

Traditional nursery nurse training (NNEB), which many of my colleagues engaged with 20–25 years ago, involved making a sizeable number of detailed written observations of a child. While this was a good discipline, when I read some of those observations, I doubt their usefulness in identifying the learning or possible next steps, which can be notoriously difficult to identify. So, if the intention is to put together a case study of a child's learning over time, then certain aspects are going to be more important than others. Chapter 4 focuses on making useful observations, depending on the purpose of the exercise. The concept of 'involvement' is introduced as a guide for when to observe or record (Laevers, 1997).

Gathering information can be 'messy'

There often comes a point when gathering observations, when you feel confused and lose focus. This is to be expected. If you are gathering enough data on which to draw for a case study, it can get 'messy' and unmanageable. It is best to let this happen. It means you are getting somewhere and also have enough data to analyse in different ways. Chapter 5 deals with the selection of the material to include, while Chapter 6 introduces some theories and frameworks you may want to use.

Analysing your observations

The analysis comes next, in Chapter 7. Analysis involves a close examination of all of the parts of your data. So, for example, if you are focusing on the learning achieved, you might consider a particular subject area and pick out where the child you observed seemed to be exploring that subject. Noticing actions over time enables you to pick out very small changes or developments. If you are focusing on the dispositions a child is using, you might have a list such as 'being curious', 'persevering', 'showing confidence', etc., and you may look out for the development of these qualities. Detailed observations might lend themselves to being analysed in different ways.

An example of an observation (by Cath Arnold)

My car was in the garage for a service. Georgia (aged 3y 9m 7d) and her mum took me to the garage. The car was not quite ready so Georgia asked to stay and wait for me. She was intrigued as to why two cars and a van were on ramps and the van was obviously higher. She asked, 'Why is the van higher?' I suggested it might be because the man working on the van was taller. When my car was lowered to the ground, she said 'The man can't fit under there now.' I said 'Only if he lies down.'

Analysis

If I was using, for example, a subject-based curriculum to think about this little conversation, I could deduce that Georgia was interested in size and, in particular, height, and could recognise differences in size. I might describe her learning in terms of mathematical development. I would watch out for further evidence of that interest.

If using a dispositional framework to think about this short observation, I could see that Georgia was developing the disposition to be curious and able to ask questions to gain information.

I could also look at my own pedagogy. It might have been more helpful to respond by asking Georgia, 'What do you think?' Whatever her response, I might have gained more insight into her thinking.

In every chapter of this book, you will see examples from observations of Georgia (Arnold, 1997: 1999). There will also be examples from other child observation studies and from the literature.

A second example of an observation (made by Jean Piaget in the Maison des Petits in order to illustrate some of the differences in children's play, and published in *Play, Dreams and Imitation* in 1951, in English)

> OBS. 70 At 5:2 V. amused himself by jumping up and down on the stairs. At first he carried out his movements aimlessly, but later he tried to jump from the ground onto a seat, increasing the distance he jumped each time.
>
> (Piaget, 1951: 117)

Analysis

V seemed to be involved in estimating the distance he could jump, so, like Georgia, he was exploring an aspect of mathematics but he was using his whole body as well as thinking about distance.

> Piaget offered this as an illustration of a 'sensory-motor practice game' carried out purely for pleasure or because the child could do it. He pointed out that we do this with any new learning.

Chapter 8 brings together Georgia's story into a coherent whole, drawing on aspects from throughout the book. The purpose of this is to demonstrate how observations gathered over time can form a coherent whole and can demonstrate learning.

The final chapter, 'Concluding thoughts', revisits and draws together the steps explored in the book.

1   Choosing a child to study

'What I know of children I have learned from them.'

(Pratt, 1948: 9)

This quote from Caroline Pratt illustrates why child study is important. We can learn from children and from each child as we observe them, so if we approach child study in an open way, thinking first that we are here to learn, this attitude really helps.

Introduction

This chapter presents ideas about:

- how children learn, drawing on constructivism and rejecting behaviourism
- who to choose to study and why
- criteria that might be used to decide who to study
- the importance of presenting each child's context
- approaching parents and engaging in an ongoing dialogue
- pitfalls when choosing who to study.

How children learn

Before deciding who to study, it is important to reflect on your beliefs about how children learn. Most of us, as adults, are informed by our own experiences and family culture. My few memories of my early childhood lead me to believe I had a level of freedom from my mum, but my dad was a lot more protective. It was no problem to make a mess in the house. In fact, my mum's philosophy was not to interrupt us if we were what she called 'occupied'. She could be described as a 'nativist' or 'laissez-faire' teacher/parent. Unlike Piaget or Darwin, my mum was not observing closely what we were doing, but was happy that she could get on with household chores while we were engaged in play.

Thinking about your early childhood and family culture

- What sorts of play can you remember becoming engaged in?
- What kinds of play were allowed? Indoors? Outdoors?
- How has this affected your attitudes to play?

(Be aware that this can bring up painful memories for some.)

As well as drawing on our memories of our own upbringing, we can also draw on what others have written, both about their experiences and about how children learn. Among the many books I have read on the subject of 'how children learn' I seem to favour the methods that provide children with a level of freedom and acknowledge children's intrinsic motivation to learn. It was many years before I realised and read about the theory of 'constructivism', and found that this way of thinking about children and how they approach learning fitted with my beliefs. Put simply, constructivism means that we construe our understanding of the world from our firsthand experiences. We 'assimilate' experiences we can make a connection with that are 'similar' to what we have come across before, and we 'accommodate' our actions and thinking to new experiences. As learners, we need to be actively involved in our learning experiences. Constructivism is a 'theory of knowing' and makes the case that the knowing is located in each of us as individuals, rather than being something separate that can be delivered (Von Glaserfeld, 1990; Proulx, 2006). I also subscribe to the idea that we learn from one another, through seeing different ways of doing things and through dialogue. This is usually referred to as 'social constructivism'. This concept acknowledges the learner as initiator of their own learning, and also other people, who contribute or support in some way, taking into account what the learner is trying to master (Vygotsky, 1978).

In contrast, 'behaviourism' seems to make the assumption that we learn because of reinforcements and rewards. Behaviourists take into account only what can be observed in the here and now, so what comes from the mind of the child or learner is not likely to be acknowledged. Behaviourists look for evidence in behaviour and make no reference to 'mental events or to internal psychological processes' (Graham, 2010: 2). So, if we hold the belief that children's actions can be explained only through what we can observe and that we, as adults, can train children to respond in particular ways and to learn through being given rewards and sanctions, then we might favour this approach. Language like 'reinforcing' behaviour is underpinned by the belief that we, as adults, control or shape the behaviour of children. Behaviourism was popular for a while early in the twentieth century and certainly used as a way to try to control the behaviour of children with additional needs, particularly autism. However, in recent years, specialists in autism have recognised that children bring their own ideas and motivations to the learning situation, and that behaviour does not depend purely on responses to the adult's actions and reinforcements.

My main problem with a behaviourist approach is that it takes little account of the child's innate drive to learn and the satisfaction derived from learning. I can also apply this to myself as an adult learner. Learning something new, especially if one has to work hard to master it, is pleasurable in itself and rewards can detract from that pleasure. Donaldson (1987: 115) points out that there are 'grave risks' to using extrinsic rewards: first, that those children who do not gain the rewards see themselves as losers; second, that offering rewards reduces children's motivation to engage in the same activities subsequently. Donaldson draws on several studies and states that 'extrinsic material reward tends to decrease enjoyment' (1987: 116).

She also makes the point that we all need 'verbal encouragement' and that this is very different to giving stars or stickers and, in fact, has the effect of encouraging children to continue and to repeat their actions (1987: 117). More recent research, by Dweck, indicates that the type of verbal encouragement can make a difference to how children respond. Offering 'learning goals' and praising effort rather than achievement encourages a 'mastery oriented' attitude to learning, whereas offering 'performance goals' and always praising only achievement can lead to a 'helpless' attitude to learning (Dweck and Leggett, 1988). Praising effort can help foster a kind of 'growth mindset' rather than a 'fixed mindset' about intelligence (Dweck, 2000).

As well as being intrinsically motivated to learn in general, I believe that children come equipped to explore their worlds using patterns of action, or 'schemas' (Athey, 2007). There is plenty of evidence to indicate that these actions are not copied or imitated but are in some way innate and yet universally explored. I find that educators with a behaviourist attitude assume that children's actions are purely imitations of what the children have observed. Obviously, children do imitate what they have seen, but in my view that is only part of the story.

Although behaviourism, in its most extreme form, has been rejected, there are many remnants of that approach in our British education system today. The balance between 'delivering' a curriculum and each child learning is often heavily weighted towards the 'delivery' of the curriculum. I have a particular distaste for the use of 'deliver' when thinking about education and learning. I believe 'delivering' something that is defined by adults to each child is misguided. An alternative way of thinking about this is to 'offer worthwhile experiences' to children that 'feed' or extend their interests (Athey, 2007). This way, you begin with the child's interests and, because this is an 'offer' rather than a requirement, children can choose whether or not to take up the offer.

Table 1.1 Main features of 'constructivism' and 'behaviourism'

(Social) Constructivism	Behaviourism
The child is an active learner 'born with the ability to adapt and to learn from the environment'	The child is a 'blank slate' and 'passive'
'Cognitive development is the result of an interaction between the individual and the environment', including people	Stimulation comes from outside Most learning comes from the teacher
'The child plays an active role in developmental change by deriving information from the environment and using it to modify existing mental structures'	'Reinforcements, like rewards, increase the likelihood of behaviour being repeated' 'Behaviour modification techniques are used'
Constructivism is a theory of knowing	

Source: Das Gupta (1994: 21–33)

Thinking about your practice and beliefs

- How do you believe that children learn?
- Which of the approaches above do you favour?
- How often do you use language like 'deliver' or 'reinforce'?
- How do you plan for children's learning?
- Can you give a rationale for planning in the way that you do?

Responding to the questions in the box may help you write about what you believe in your account of your child study.

In her introduction to *Children in the Nursery School*, which was written in 1928, Harriett Johnson spends three chapters outlining how the staff believe that children learn, how the teachers deal with habits and conventions, and how the environment and daily schedule are arranged (Johnson, 1928/72). Her philosophy, in an experimental school for children under 3, is to allow for experimentation following children's interests and making only appropriate demands on children – for example, rather than insisting on children saying 'please' and 'thank you' before they have an understanding of what those words mean, the adults treat the children with respect, using language as they would with other adults. Gradually children adopt those conventions. The children are aged 14 months to 3 years, and the book contains photos of children using the equipment and sketches of their block building, which adds another dimension to the information offered to the reader. In this instance, the illustrations add to the descriptions of the setting and activities. I often find that degree participants put photos into their assignments without thinking carefully about whether the illustrations actually add anything to their accounts. Perhaps they are added at the last minute to make the work look more attractive. If we are writing about something a child has done, often a sequence of photos tells the story more clearly than a single snapshot.

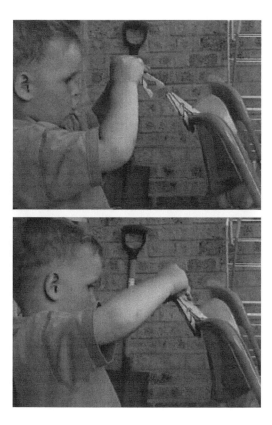

Figure 1.1 Example of a sequence of two photos: Harry connecting with pegs

Who to study

If you are embarking on the study of a single child over a short period of time, you need to consider choosing a child that you have regular access to. You need to have some interest in that child. They may be playing in a way that puzzles or intrigues you. We are drawn towards children for different reasons. As a female worker, you may want to understand boys' play and choose a child who plays in a very active way or, as a male worker, you may want to extend your knowledge of play typically associated with girls. If you are an early years teacher in training, you may need to study a younger age group than you will teach in order to study child development.

Engaging with their parents is another essential feature. So, if you find parents that are interested (and in my experience this is most parents) then your study is more likely to be valuable and not superficial. In traditional positivist research, you would be seeking to be 'objective', defined by the dictionary as 'free of bias'. However, the very nature of child study means that you become involved with the child and family over at least the period of your study and it is usually impossible to be objective. Rinaldi, writing about practice in the world-renowned Reggio Emilia nurseries in northern Italy, argues that 'there is no objective point of view that can make observation neutral' (2006: 128). We simply cannot be objective when carrying out observations. We are always interpreting what we see through our own experiences. We make decisions about what to watch, for how long, and how to record and to share what we are seeing. Discussing with parents what you have observed offers you the opportunity of their insights into their own child's learning. So, observing is always subjective, but it can also be done with rigour. The rigour comes from observing and recording in some detail near, in time, to the event you are describing, and in a way that initial judgements are not made, and also from giving the child's exact age in each observation, so that progress can be clearly identified by the reader.

If your study is of more than one child and over an extended period – for example, a dissertation period, which may be six months to a year or more – then the above also applies. If you are choosing three or four children, you may want a gender balance. Although single-child and small studies cannot claim to be representative of the whole population, you may gain insights into how different children engage.

Criteria you might use to choose a child for a short child study (over a few weeks)

- A child whose parent(s) you already know
- A child who you will see regularly over that period (perhaps he and his family attend a group you run or you are his key person in nursery)
- A child with whom you have built some trust
- A child who gets involved easily and is not put off by the camera (if you are filming)
- A child whose play interests you

Table 1.2 Examples of criteria used when children are chosen to study

Topic	Criteria for selecting participants
'Children who play together have similar schemas' (dissertation for a diploma)	In order to engage all staff, we chose seven nursery children; four were boys and three were girls. The age range was 2y 10m to 4y. Each Family Worker had at least one child involved in the study, who would be observed at home by their parents and at nursery by their Family Workers. In addition, we chose one girl of 4y 8m, who was about to go to primary school, and one boy of 15m. These two were the children of staff who would be observed at home. Our idea was to involve the whole team alongside a team of parents, in the investigation. (Children were observed during three separate weeks.)
'Understanding young children and their contexts for learning: building on early experience' (MEd study)	The four focus children were two boys and two girls ranging in age from 2y 6m to 3y 3m at the beginning of the study. Their family make-up was different, i.e. M was an only child of a single mother, who attended nursery full-time; G was an older sibling with a younger brother living with two parents, who attended nursery part-time; C was the youngest child of three, with two parents, who attended nursery part-time; L was the youngest of four, with a mother and stepfather, who attended nursery full-time. We were seeking a gender balance and diversity in family make-up, not to really represent the nursery population, but to discover how four unique families supported their children's learning at home and how we could build on those home experiences. (Children were observed at home by their parents and at nursery over a period of 18 months.)
'Young children's representations of emotions and attachment in their spontaneous patterns of behaviour: an exploration of a researcher's understanding' (PhD study)	Two children, a boy and a girl, were chosen for the pilot study on the basis of their parents' interest. Four more children were chosen for the main study, three girls and one boy. The main criteria was parents' interest and likely cooperation. All but one of the families were known to me prior to the study. Data on one more girl was included because of the nature of her play, which offered insights into the topic under investigation. Children were studied and filmed over one to two years, and regular discussions were held with their workers and parents. The researcher kept a learning journal of her reflections on the process.

Note: All of the above studies were carried out at the Pen Green Centre in collaboration with staff and parents

A rationale for choosing

A rationale for choosing can consist of many different reasons, but I have found I learn most from children who become involved or engaged, even when I am around. There is always the danger that your study interrupts children's play and I would want to avoid this at all costs. Depending on the children's ages, and your relationship with them, I would want to involve them in deciding whether and how involved they become. Kate Hayward gives a delightful account of meeting John for the first time and gaining his permission for a small study (Hayward, 2012: 125). John was 4 years old at the time and could understand that Kate was going into his school to study his and other children's emerging writing. He opted to 'draw a strawberry' rather than write his name to give permission. This was his own idea and showed that he was exercising some autonomy in this situation. The point here is not that John did a drawing, but that he substituted it for writing his name, which he was able to do at that time but chose not to. It is best to be flexible and not to decide in advance how you will gain permission from children. Children will also share how they feel about you observing them on each occasion by welcoming you and seeming pleased to see you, or by turning away or walking away, or just looking really uncomfortable. One girl I studied, on one occasion, went inside a play tent and did the zip up, which was a clear signal to me to stop what I was doing and move away.

You may opt to study your own child, or a relative or friend's child, who you already feel that you know well. You still need to think very carefully about whether the child you have chosen is the right age, whether you will enhance your relationship with them and who the other adults will be who will be willing to become involved in the study. In a way, you and the other adults who are in dialogue about the observations you have made are interpreting what you see and making meaning together about this child's learning. So, even if you are studying your own child, seeking interpretations from other adults, close to that child, is part of the study. Children do not grow up in isolation so the context of their family and culture is relevant and, nowadays, usually that is given in some detail at the beginning of any written study.

In *Play, Dreams and Imitation*, written in 1945, Piaget acknowledged that he was using observations of his own three children from birth, but he gave no real context other than what was contained in the observation itself. He began by saying:

> We will begin with the few observations we have been able to make with regard to our own children:
>
> OBS. 1. On the very night after his birth, T. was wakened by the babies in the nearby cots and began to cry in chorus with them.

He goes on to discuss whether this is imitation or 'merely the starting off of a reflex by an external stimulus', and also whether T. could differentiate between the cries of the other babies and his own cries (1951: 7). He also makes comparisons between his children, noting that 'J. developed more slowly than her brother and sister' (1951: 10).

Liz Brooker studied 16 children and gave the context of each child and family near to the beginning of her book, *Starting School* (2002: 2). Brooker gives some general history, i.e. 'half of the children were "Anglo" … the remaining from Bangladeshi homes', and then goes on to introduce each family in more detail, including whether parents were working and, in some cases, the parents' school experiences. Here are two examples:

> **Troy** was the oldest child of Charlotte, a mother who was taking her life into her own hands and refashioning it. Charlotte had spent her childhood in a series of foster homes, with frequent changes of school. After separating from her first partner, the father of Troy and his brother Jerome, she had met and married Bob, and set out to attain a life of respectability and esteem. Her ambition was to give her children a 'perfect life' to compensate for her own childhood unhappiness.
>
> (Brooker, 2002: 4)

> Abu Bokkar lived across the street from Khiernssa, and his mother Rahena was friends with Minara. Bokkar was the seventh and youngest child in the family, and was seen as special by his parents, who nicknamed him 'little prince'. His father, who was unemployed, was an educated man, involved in the Bangladeshi community at many levels, and very conscious of his children's educational progress. Their family life appeared to revolve around the children's schooling, and the requirements of mosque school; all their hopes were tied up in their children's future.
>
> (Brooker, 2002: 4)

Although there are similarities between these two families, in that both were focused on their children's futures, as the stories of starting school unfold we see that there are many differences too.

Introducing Georgia

Introducing Georgia's context

As Georgia will feature throughout this book, this is how I gave her context when I wrote about her in my master's study, completed in 1997. Notice that, like Piaget, I use only the initial of her first name. I would not do that now, or advise it, as it is very hard to relate to a child without a name. If anonymity is required, participants can choose a pseudonym, which is further explored in Chapter 2.

Figure 1.2 Photos of Georgia in the garden, aged 17 months

At the beginning of the study period, G (aged 2 years 11 months) was living with her two parents and younger brother (aged 7 months). Her father's family originally came from Scotland and her mother's family came from other parts of England. Several members of the extended family lived in the local area. G's interests at home, according to her parents, were 'being mummy' and feeding her dolls. Her parents hoped that attending playgroup and then nursery would help her to become independent and confident, get used to being with other children and play with more messy things than at home. Her favourite stories were 'Gorilla', 'The Tiger who came to Tea' and 'Fireman Sam'. Songs she liked were '5 Fat Sausages', 'Incy, Wincy Spider' and 'Wheels on the Bus'. Her important people were her maternal grandparents, aunt and uncle, and older children in the small circular close where the family lived, particularly nine year old twins, Jennifer and Amy.

As you can see, this is a brief picture of Georgia at the beginning of the study period, when I was telling the reader what was considered relevant. I did not mention that Georgia was my granddaughter, mainly because my editor advised me not to. By the time *Observing Harry* was published (four years later and with a different editor), I was encouraged to write about my relationship with him both at home and at nursery. So you, too, may receive conflicting advice or find that things change over time.

Approaching the child's parents

A critical part of the process of engaging in child study is approaching the parents of the child you want to study. I always begin with the assumption that the study will be of benefit to them and their child. However, you do have to bear in mind that not only are you asking to study their child, either in nursery (your workplace) or at their home, but also that you are asking for a commitment from them. It helps if you have thought this through and are able to outline at the outset how you hope they will be involved. Depending on the piece of work you are undertaking, you may want to meet and talk two or three times over a four-week period; you may want monthly meetings over a longer period; you may suggest that they keep a diary or video recording of their child's play at home to put together with the data you are gathering. All or any of this puts additional pressure on already busy families. It may be better to ask how they would like to be involved and to make a plan together as this acknowledges their commitments, too. If you are prepared to do things on their terms, which may involve visits to their home at times that suit them or arranging childcare for their children in the setting, so you can have an uninterrupted meeting with them in your workplace, you are more likely to be successful.

Depending on how well you know the parents at this point, you may have to reassure them as to why you have chosen their child. Parents often worry about their child's development and if a request to study their child comes out of the blue they may assume that there is a problem with their child's development. So it is well worth writing down your reasons for choosing their child, which you would need to do anyway for a written assignment.

Children or families that opt in

Another approach can be to offer an invitation to all families to become involved in your study. The difficulty with this approach is that either no one may respond or several parents may respond and then may be disappointed if not chosen. I favour the more personal approach, which involves choosing a child or children (who fit the criteria for the study) and then approaching their parents. Occasionally parents will ask if they can take part and I would usually try to accommodate them if possible as it is always helpful to have willing volunteers and they are likely to commit time to the study. Occasionally children will volunteer, as illustrated in the following example.

Observing Harry

When *Child Development and Learning 2–5 Years: Georgia's Story* was published, I was very excited as it was my first book to be published and it was an in-depth study of my granddaughter, based partly on a case study I had written as part of my master's degree study. By then Georgia was 8 and her brother Harry was 6. When the proofs had arrived a few weeks earlier, Georgia and Harry read what they considered the 'funny bits' to each other. Harry would say, 'I'll be Dad and you be Paul', and they would laugh very loudly at what I had written.

We had a party at home to celebrate, to which I invited my friends and work colleagues. That evening Harry asked, 'Will you have a party at home to celebrate when you write a book about me?' I said I would if I could. He kept asking whenever I saw him: 'When will you write the book about me?' Luckily his parents and I had made detailed notes and had filmed Harry during his early years. Along with his 'Celebration of Achievement' from Pen Green Nursery, we had quite a bit of raw data. Eventually I wrote a proposal and approached a publisher, who turned it down. Then I bought an author's handbook in order to find out which other publishers to approach. The second publisher accepted my proposal with some changes …

… and we did have a party at home to celebrate the publication of *Observing Harry: Child Development and Learning 0–5 Years*. By then Harry was 10.

Harry thought it was only fair that he have a book about him, like his sister did (and a party to celebrate!). In this case Harry was old enough to be consulted and to give his permission for what was written.

Organising an ongoing dialogue

Your initial approach to parents is very important, but so is continuing the dialogue over time, whether that is a few weeks or months. As I have already mentioned, it helps to have some sort of plan put together with the parents about where, when and how frequently you meet up and talk. It must be geared towards what they can manage comfortably and not be a burden to them or, indeed, too onerous for you. I have always found that sharing photos or video footage really attracts parents, and that is so much easier to do now with the technological advances. Video material in particular allows you and the parent(s) to have a say about what you think the child's experience is and means, in terms of their learning. Five minutes of film is actually quite a long time and needs to be watched in real time, and you may both/all want to see it more than once. So it is well worth capturing a really good piece to share. Ideas about tools and techniques will be discussed in Chapter 3.

What are the pitfalls when choosing who to study?

If you choose to study a child who attends a setting in which you work, the greatest risk is that they will not attend regularly enough for you to gather enough data for a study. If yours is a single-child study and you are not able to gather enough data, you may have to choose another child to study. It is difficult to define what 'enough' data is, as sometimes we have a bit of luck and gather data that is quite rich near the beginning of a study. At other times, we have to observe for longer periods and build a trusting relationship with a child before we begin to gather rich data. When I mention 'rich' data, I mean when a child is absorbed in play either alone or with others. That deep absorption is a sign that they are learning and not too inhibited by your presence. In Chapter 4, the concept of 'involvement' and 'deep level learning' is discussed (Laevers, 1997).

For my master's study, I chose to study four children, two boys and two girls, alongside their parents, over a period of 18 months. During the first six months I collected very little data on one girl, who had sporadic attendance at nursery. At that point, I reviewed the material gathered and made the decision to include my granddaughter, Georgia, who was just starting to attend nursery at that time and with whom I had been piloting some methods of observation at home. I had to explain to the family of the other girl that I was not continuing to study her because of her attendance. I think they appreciated my honesty and they were given the small amount of data gathered to date. Had that been a single-child study, I would have had to act a lot more quickly or maybe have a contingency plan, so it is worth thinking through what you would do in any of these circumstances.

Another risk is that your presence inhibits the child's play and they do not become involved while you are observing them. Putting the camera on a tripod or shelf can alleviate this problem as, once you begin interacting with them as you usually would, they may become less self-conscious about the camera. However, this is a tricky decision, as I would find it unethical to 'trick' a child in any way, into thinking they were not being filmed. So you must ensure that they know you are filming and give their permission.

One issue that has come up for me, on more than one occasion, is a child's interest in the camera. I have found it almost impossible to film a child who shows a strong and persistent interest in the camera I am using. The only solution to this is to use a second camera to film their explorations with the camera. Ultimately, and if necessary, you may have to choose a different child to study.

Sometimes children leave unexpectedly for a variety of reasons. If this is 'mid-study' for you, make sure, whenever possible, that you can stay in contact with the parents to gain final permissions. I have known people begin to study a second child mid-study and write up their learning from both children, which is feasible.

If you choose to study your own child or a close relative or friend's child, then the chances are that they will stick with you. There are different risks involved. You may take some of the things they do for granted. You need to 'make the familiar strange' in order to keep a close record of their actions, relationships and whatever else is of interest (Nutbrown, 2012). It is a good idea to have a critical friend, who can look at your data, to find out what they see. If you are not studying your own child, you will be discussing the data with the parent.

Issues to consider

- Will I have enough access to this child to study him/her over this period of study?
- Am I clear about why I have chosen him/her?
- Are his/her parents able to be involved?
- Have I a plan that will enable me to carry out enough observations and meet with the adults important to this child?
- Do I need a contingency plan?

2 Considering the ethical aspects of child study

The UN Convention on the Rights of the Child (1989) includes:

Article 3: The best interests of children must be the primary concern in making decisions that may affect them.

Article 29: Children's education should develop each child's personality, talents and abilities to the fullest.

I quote from the UN Convention, as carrying out a child observation study requires students and researchers to both act in the best interests of children, with regard to their rights, and enhance or improve their educational opportunities. Therefore these statements are very much in tune with our aims when carrying out a child observation study.

Introduction

This chapter discusses:

- what is ethics, and how can we be sure of behaving ethically
- what is special about research with children
- what we mean by 'co-constructing' meaning
- examples of thinking through the ethics of a study
- behaving ethically when studying babies.

What is ethics?

Dictionary definitions of 'ethics' include 'that branch of philosophy that is concerned with human character and behaviour', 'professional standards of conduct' and 'rules of behaviour' (Kirkpatrick, 1983: 432). Ethics are to do with how we behave in our interactions with others. Tulloch defines 'ethics' as 'rules of conduct', and relates ethics to 'ethos', defined as 'the characteristic spirit or attitudes of a community' (1993: 505). I find the link with 'ethos' helpful as I believe much of *how* we do things and conduct ourselves with others is to do with our attitudes. If we see other adults as equal to us, then surely we want to listen to and include their views. If we want to convey a fair account of a child's learning, we must watch and listen to them carefully, picking up on their body signals and any signs that they are uncomfortable with being observed by us.

When it comes to research, our responsibility is to think through, in advance, what the risks or pitfalls might be. It is very much thinking about *how* we do things, rather than what we do.

Before the late 1980s and the early 1990s very little was written about ethics in research methodology books. Following the Nuremberg Trials after the Second World War and the Thalidomide disaster of the late 1950s, the general public were aware of ethics in relation to medical research, but this was not automatically or immediately transferred to social research (Aubrey *et al.*, 2000: 159). By the late 1990s and early in the 2000s, most books on research methodology included a section or chapter on ethics. Common themes include: informed consent, anonymity, confidentiality and the right to withdraw. These are all tricky to achieve, especially among small populations and in relation to children.

How can we be sure we are behaving ethically?

Informed consent

This means that anyone participating in research should understand, at the outset, what the research is about, what their involvement is likely to be, how the data will be analysed, how the findings will be written up and with whom they will be shared, before they give written consent for a researcher to embark on a study. Often the researcher finds it difficult to articulate for themselves what the likely outcomes are, so explaining every angle to another person can be difficult. With regard to young children, efforts must be made to explain to them in a way that they can grasp what is likely to happen. Usually researchers seek the consent of the parents, who act as 'gatekeepers' on their children's behalf. They then seek the 'assent' of children by providing information they can understand and negotiating some way of them agreeing at the outset, like John's original idea of 'drawing a strawberry' (Hayward, 2012), discussed in Chapter 1. For very young children, we have to rely on our powers of observation and never allow the research to take precedence over their general well-being as observed in the moment.

Anonymity

Most guidance states that anonymity should be offered to participants. They can choose a pseudonym for you to use in any written work. Universities seem to favour this approach but, in my view, it is not quite as simple as it seems. For a start, if you are working in collaboration with the parents of the child you are studying, a sign of them feeling like real collaborators is for their names to be included, as well as yours. A way around this, is to provide a copy with real names for the participants plus family and close friends to keep, but to use pseudonyms in the copy submitted as an assignment. In much of my published work, I have used the real first names of children, unless I consider the material to be sensitive in any way. Considering how that child will feel and possibly react when reading about themselves later on, helps when making those sorts of decisions. Nowadays many studies include photos and filmed material so anonymity is almost impossible to achieve.

Confidentiality

Very closely linked to the idea of anonymity is the participant's right for what they tell you or what you observe to be kept confidential, unless they agree to it being shared more widely. Again, this is something that really needs thinking about as different people may have different ideas about what confidentiality means for them in their situation. As a worker, you also need to be clear that, if you discover any safeguarding issues, you must always follow procedures and act in the best interests of the child. Any agreements with parents should include that proviso. It is a bit trickier with workers, who may come into the frame and be your colleagues, or you may be their line manager. You do have a responsibility to feed back to them whatever you have observed or filmed. If that includes what you consider 'poor practice', then that needs to be done sensitively and in a context where they can feel open to discuss and learn from their observed or filmed actions. There is a lot of scope for learning from seeing ourselves on film, but most of us are reluctant to be in the frame in the first place.

I found, in one study I carried out, that I was a lot more careful to talk to parents, as individuals, about the study and the possible ethical issues, but that I treated my colleagues as a team, when actually different people had different views about being filmed and how I should go about feeding back. This taught me that it is not good enough to treat any adults as a group when dealing with sensitive issues. They actually felt less powerful in the process than the parents, who I had been very careful to treat as individuals.

The right to withdraw

Anyone can withdraw at any point, and for any reason, in the process of carrying out a child observation study. The participants need to be informed of this. Also, it is good practice to provide a named person that they can go to, to discuss their worries or concerns about the study or your conduct. They also need to be reassured that, if they withdraw or complain, there will be no impact on the service they or their child receive from you. It is rare, in my experience, for anyone to withdraw partway through a study, but it is critical that families know that they have that right. In a way, their right to withdraw protects the researcher, as it means you have to hold that possibility in mind when interacting with the participants.

Following a code of ethics

Most organisations or universities have a 'code of ethics'. Many degree participants believe that all they have to do in their written work is to include the code of ethics and state that they are adhering to it. However, it is not quite that simple. What you must do, is demonstrate *how* you are adhering to the code. So, for example, if I were embarking on my study of Georgia again using the four headings above, I would need to note the following information under each of them.

Informed consent

- I had talked through what the study was an investigation of, with her parents (building on home learning at nursery)
- I had asked them to keep a diary of her activities at home over an 18-month period and had asked whether they felt able to do this
- I had shared with them my idea of filming her at nursery for three to five minutes once a week, selecting one clip as a focus for discussion with them every three months, and had asked whether they would both be available to do that
- I had talked through with Georgia that I would be writing down and sometimes filming what she did at nursery and when she came to my house, and that she seemed pleased by my interest. I had told her I would be showing my tutor and the other nursery workers, as well as her parents. I would still look out for days when her general well-being was a bit low and make the decision on the day

Anonymity

- I was going to preserve her anonymity by not naming her but just using the first letter of her first name (and subsequently using her first name in the book I wrote about her development and learning)
- I had made the point that it is difficult to anonymise when filming and using photos, but I would always negotiate with the family when sharing film or photos more widely

Confidentiality

- As with any other family, I had informed the parents that child protection procedures would be followed if necessary
- I agreed that they, and the other parents whose children I was studying, would be involved in interpreting and deciding what material to include
- They would be made aware of where material was stored
- I also gave them copies of all filmed material

Right to withdraw

- It had been explained to them that they had a right to withdraw from the study at any time, for any reason, and that they would not suffer as a result
- Our relationship would take precedence over all else apart from a child protection issue. If Georgia's parents decided to withdraw, we would not let that act affect our relationship

Codes of ethics

Several codes of ethics are available online, including that of the British Psychological Society (BPS), the American Psychological Association (APA) and the British Educational Research Association (BERA). These organisations tend to have a list of principles to which they adhere. Apart from what is mentioned above, they emphasise 'Respect for the autonomy and dignity of persons' and 'Maximising benefit and minimising harm' (BPS, 2010: 7). Honesty and integrity in reporting on research is also highly valued (APA, 2010), as is the value of the piece of research being undertaken. The idea is that anyone who engages in research activity is contributing to their field of study and that they should conduct themselves with integrity.

What is special about research with children?

A major issue is the power differential between professionals and parents, and between adults and children. Several books and papers have been written about research with children – for example, Aubrey *et al.* (2000), David (1998), Greig and Taylor (1999), MacNaughton and Hughes (2009), and Christensen and James (2000) – while others touch on the subject (Dahlberg, Moss and Pence, 1999). Scott makes the point that 'The ethics that apply to interviewing children need, if anything, to be more stringent than with adults. Children are relatively powerless in society and despite the attention given to children's rights, have relatively little recourse to official channels of complaint' (2000: 114).

Roberts, in the same book, says that, 'It cannot be taken for granted that more listening means more hearing' (2000: 229), so merely claiming that we are 'listening to children' is not enough. We need to illustrate that we are 'hearing' what they tell us, through their actions as well as their words. Roberts goes on to state that we should be 'involving children in the process' (2000: 230). This idea is further developed by Woodhead and Faulkner, who say that, 'Significant knowledge gains result when children's active participation in the research process is deliberately solicited and when their perspectives, views and feelings are accepted as genuine, valid evidence' (2000: 31).

So we are not just talking about children's cooperation but their active involvement in sharing with researchers what they think. Woodhead and Faulkner discuss the 'social change' that has resulted in seeing children as 'participants in research rather than subjects (or objects) of research' (2000: 31). They also point out the danger that, in seeing children as competent participators, adults might take less responsibility for ensuring that children are treated ethically.

In a critical review of gaining access to the worlds and homes of young children, Murray reports that, despite believing that young children can be competent researchers, there are a number of barriers, in the form of gate-keepers such as setting leaders, who may not be open to outsiders spending time in their setting (2011). If, however, researchers do gain access, then they need to spend some considerable time participating in the life of the setting in order to 'assuage practitioners' anxieties' (2011: 97). The sharing of your observation notes with setting staff also helps with building trust, as does the inclusion of practitioners' comments as part of the data collection.

What do we mean by 'co-constructing meaning'?

First, I want to draw on Freire's conceptualisation of 'dialogue', whereby individuals engage in a two-way conversation *as equals* in order to come, together, to a fresh understanding of an aspect of the world (1996). Freire resists the idea of education as a transmission of ideas from someone who knows to someone less knowledgeable. So teachers learn from children as well as children learning from teachers.

Second, in applying this idea to young children, we need to think about our 'image of the child' as workers in Reggio Emilia and at Pen Green have done, in their 'Making Children's Learning Visible' (MCLV) project (Rinaldi, 2006; Hayward and McKinnon, 2014). Rinaldi describes how the Reggio team view learning:

> Learning does not take place by means of transmission or reproduction. It is a process of construction, in which each individual constructs for himself the reasons, the 'whys', the meanings of things, others, nature, events, reality and life. The learning process

is certainly individual, but because the reasons, explanations, interpretations and meanings of others are indispensable for our knowledge building, it is also a process of relations – a process of social construction. We thus consider knowledge to be a process of construction by the individual in relation with others, a true act of co-construction.

(2006: 125)

Rinaldi goes on to describe school as 'a place of research, where the children, along with the teachers, are the primary researchers' (2006: 125). 'Listening' and being open to the ideas of children becomes essential, if, like the Reggio team, you see children as 'strong, powerful and rich in potential and resources, right from the moment of birth', which is how they describe their image of the child (Rinaldi, 2006: 123).

I want to emphasise that the 'image of the child' may be evolving, but, because it is based on our deeply held beliefs and values, it is likely to have certain features that do not change a great deal over time. Hayward and McKinnon (2014: 69) draw our attention to what was written by Pen Green parents and staff more than 30 years ago:

The Pen Green Curriculum Document, written in 1983, stated that at Pen Green we encourage children

- To feel strong
- To feel in control
- To feel able to question
- To feel able to choose

A similar exercise carried out in 2010 by a group of Pen Green staff engaging in the MCLV project along with other nursery schools produced the following statements.

This group wanted children to be

- Confident and strong
- Able to question
- Able to choose
- Able to assert themselves
- Empathetic
- Secure

(Hayward and McKinnon, 2014: 70)

So, although participants in this exercise were different people, the values and image of the child are similar. This idea of negotiating a shared image of the child builds on the process of sharing values and beliefs as described in the introduction.

If we are clear that we are prepared to actively listen to children's ideas, then we can actually learn from them and co-construct with them a record of their learning over time, which is shared. Dahlberg (in Dahlberg *et al.*, 1999: 51–52) gives a personal account of an experience she had in Reggio Emilia, which prompted her to realise that she was not always listening to her son when he was imploring her to buy him another He-Man figure she did not approve of. I wonder how often, as parents and workers, we ignore children's interests in favour of something we consider more worthwhile. Part of behaving ethically is to listen to children and understand what is of concern or interest to them.

Examples of thinking through the ethics of a study

We have seen that, historically, ethics were not considered terribly important in social research, or not important enough to warrant writing about. So it was interesting for me to look at how different writers and researchers have dealt with ethical issues, even though this was done implicitly rather than explicitly. The three examples below are longitudinal studies carried out by parents on their own children.

The Development of Scientific Concepts in a Young Child: A Case Study (a single-child study, 1955)

Navarra, writing in 1955 as he embarked on the study of his son, highlights that 'the observation should be systematic' (1955: 6); that 'direct quotations of a child's verbalizations' are helpful (1955: 7); and he quotes 'Bohn from a 1916 study', saying that 'the most fruitful situation for a [child] study would be the free play activities in which a child becomes engaged during his day-to-day living in a family setting' (1955: 8). Navarra felt there was a need to observe his son, who was referred to as L.B. (Little Boy) throughout, 24 hours a day, and therefore that L.B.'s mother should act as co-investigator, with some train-ing, which involved both parents observing him and comparing notes. When setting up the investigation to study *The Development of Scientific Concepts in a Young Child*, Navarra writes:

> ... the purpose and intent of the present investigation was to provide for naïve and discerning observation unfettered by preconceived hypotheses. This seemed implicit in the major emphasis placed on the study of the actual spontaneous behaviour of the child; and, further, it seemed clear that inferences should be drawn solely from what the child was seen to do and say.
>
> (1955: 29)

This seems to imply that the observers acted with **integrity**, being open to what would be revealed, and without preconceived ideas about what they would find. Play was important to L.B. and to the study: 'The study of play activity became the most important device by which insight was gained concerning the conceptual development of the child. However, it should be stressed that no undue attempt was made to control the conditions under which the child operated and played' (1955: 29).

This statement implies that L.B. led his own play and that what was reported was **authentic** and **honest**. The parents tried to 'build confidence' by offering freedom and security. Their attitude was important. Navarra gives a flavour of the attitude they adopted:

> L.B. and all of the children who were studied in the process of play-ing with him seemed to be eager to have someone listen to them …
> The investigators were careful to have L.B. understand that they were willing to aid him in his undertakings … He was encouraged to think aloud but the observers never insisted that he communicate … One might say that the investigators learned not to pressure the child into telling or giving an explanation about anything … On the few occa-sions when he was put on the spot, superficial replies were obtained.
>
> (1955: 30)

Navarra sums it up thus: 'On the whole, the role of the investigator was to be present, interested, and helpful, but definitely not "nosy" or domineering' (1955: 31). This suggests to me that what L.B.'s parents were doing was **maxi-mising the benefits to him**. They also emphasise that they were 'honest' with him and that 'L.B. was at all times fully aware that the record was being made' (1955: 32). This seems to constitute **informed consent**. By referring to him as L.B. throughout, it could be argued that they preserved **anonymity**. On the other hand, it was fairly clear that he was their son, so anonymity was difficult to establish although Navarra tended to refer to him as either L.B. or 'the child' so maybe it is only in retrospect that their relationship seems obvious.

Gnys at Wrk: A Child Learns to Write and Read (a single-child study, 1980)

Glenda Bissex studied her son Paul's development of writing and reading from ages 5–11. Her study was less intentional to begin with: 'When I began taking notes about my infant son's development, I did not know I was gather-ing "data" for "research"; I was a mother with a propensity for writing things down' (1980: v).

Bissex found that, through writing things down, she became more inter-ested in the strategies Paul used, and in his own invented spellings. She was 'an English teacher just retrained in reading' and was 'particularly interested in her son's language development' (1980: v).

Bissex gives a description of the case study method: 'A case study is essentially an attempt to understand another person through enlightened subjectivity, which seeks both to share the experience of another and to reflect upon it from a distance' (1980: vi).

She points out that 'Parent-researchers may be long on sharing and short on distancing' (1980: vi), so if we accept the definition of case study above, Bissex means that parents are inevitably very close to their own children, which makes it more difficult to distance themselves to gain any unbiased view, but the insights they gain can be widely shared.

Bissex mentions no agreement at the outset, but Paul was of an age to make a choice about being involved. This is how she describes what happened: 'At the beginning, Paul was an unconscious subject, unaware of the significance of my tape recorder and notebook. When he first became aware, at about age six, he was pleased by my interest and attention' (1980: vii).

So it does not seem that she tried to explain what she was doing. It was just part of life that Paul's mother was interested in his progress. She continues:

> By seven, he had become an observer of his own progress. When I worked on my initial analysis of the first year's data (5:1–6:1) and had Paul's early writings spread out on my desk, he loved to look at them with me and try to read them … About this same time Paul had observed me writing down a question he had asked about spelling, and I enquired how he felt about my writing it down. 'Then I know that when I'm older I can see the stuff I asked when I was little,' he commented.
>
> (1980: vii)

So, he did give a sort of **informed consent**. However, things changed and:

> At eight he was self-conscious enough to object to obvious observation and note-taking, which I then stopped. One day when I was making informal observations of his laterality, he looked at my notebook to see what I was jotting down and said, 'I don't like to be charted on everything I do' (8:0). Paul still brought his writings (except personal ones) to me, sharing my sense of their importance.
>
> (1980: vii)

Here he was exercising some choice in what was documented and more aware that he wanted some **confidentiality** around what was used for the study. Bissex does not explain what 'informal observations' means. She goes on to explain that, 'At nine he became a participant in the research, interested in thinking about *why* he had written or read things as he once had' (1980: vii).

She summed up by stating that, 'The study has become a special bond between us, an interest we share in each other's work, a mutual enjoyment of Paul's early childhood and of his growing up. I have come to appreciate certain qualities in my son that I might not have seen except through the eyes of this study' (1980: viii).

It could be argued that Bissex did not formally seek 'informed consent' or 'assent' from Paul, however the fact that he objected at certain points but still wanted to contribute, seems to indicate that things are more complex than they seem. The initial consent given, either by parents or children, always needs checking at certain key points during the study. I would suggest gaining consent: (1) at the outset; (2) during the gathering of data (on each occasion where children are involved); and (3) during and after writing up. The more that children and their parents can be involved in the process with you, the more ethical the study becomes.

Drawing and Painting: Children and Visual Representation, 2nd edn (a longitudinal study of three children plus many other short studies, 2003)

John Matthews studied his own 'three children, Benjamin, Joel and Hannah, from birth till they were teenagers' (2003: 5). Although he does not explicitly mention ethics, his whole approach is about supporting children's creativity and introducing the reader to a different conceptualisation of art from the art normally recognised in schools. Matthews is a strong advocate for children, believing that 'they use anything they can get their hands on for the purposes of expression and representation' (2003: 3). He argues that:

> At present there is a downplaying of children's spontaneous drawing. This is the kind of drawing children produce, with great intensity, by and for themselves; drawing which serves their own intentions, and through which they understand the world. Such drawing is essential to children's intellectual and emotional development ...
>
> (2003: 3)

Matthews very obviously began with the intention of **maximising the benefits** for his children and many others. He acknowledges that his children 'were privileged in the sense of having access to art materials and parents who are skilled and interested in drawing and painting as well as knowledgeable about child development' (2003: 5).

In describing his methodology, Matthews says that he 'chose to design naturalistic methods which captured what the children themselves were interested in and trying to draw' (2003: 7). He was interested in what the children did spontaneously and tried to be 'unobtrusive' in gathering the data. He notes, 'I do not try to distance myself from my subjects, either, but usually interact with them and talk to them. So my own interaction forms part of the data' (2003: 7).

So the whole impression we get from Matthews' account is that he is trying to promote the idea of children's expression in their own way, over which **they have control**. Also, he is dealing with a situation as near to natural as he can make it. The fact that he gathered so many examples demonstrates that the children were encouraged by their parents' interest.

Reflecting on ideas from these earlier studies

- How can I ensure that the child(ren) in my study feel in control?
- How can I maximise the benefits to the child(ren) I am studying?
- What are my thoughts about confidentiality and anonymity?
- How might I act with integrity?
- How can I be unobtrusive when carrying out observations?

Behaving ethically when studying babies

What seems a very special case is the study of babies. Inevitably, some researchers will embark on a study of a baby who is weeks or months old, and issues like 'informed consent' may seem not to apply. However, the concept of 'assent' applies even to very young babies, who will turn away when they feel overwhelmed. The important aspect is to be tuned in to how they are feeling and to look out for the tiniest signs of discomfort (Stern, 2003). Adults can give 'informed consent' on behalf of children, because they can understand what will happen and at least some of the implications, so they are agreeing with knowledge of what may happen. Children and especially very young children can only give 'assent' or agreement in the moment related to what is happening to them. They can also 'dissent', or disagree, so this is what researchers of young children must watch out for. De Lourdes Levy, Larcher and Kurz (2003: 630) point out that, 'Children are right owners even if they are not able to express their rights.' Coercion should never be used when involving children in research.

The Tavistock Method

There are examples of baby observations in the literature, some of which are made using the Tavistock Method. The Tavistock Method involves the close observation of a baby, usually at home, from birth, for an hour once a week, for the first two years. The observer tries to be open to the feelings of the baby. No notes are taken during the hour, but detailed notes are made from memory afterwards. There is no analysis, just a record of what is remembered and felt by the observer. The observations are presented and discussed in small-group seminars with fellow course participants and a tutor. The purpose is 'to study the development of babies within the family' and to be open to the feelings evoked in us as adults (Reid, 1997: 2). Unlike the sorts of child observation studies carried out for other academic courses, the observations are not shared with the parents, although the parents give permission for the study and are present and part of the whole context when observations are made, and could withdraw their consent at any time for any reason.

Other observers of infants

Charles Fernyhough closely observed his daughter, Athena, for her first three years of life. As a psychologist and a father he brings something extra special to his account (2008). He recounts what happened when Athena realised he had been studying her for three years:

> 'What are you writing?' she said.
>
> I looked up from the crowded pages of my notebook. I'd been unaware that, once again, my observations of the thing had distracted me from the thing itself.
>
> 'I'm writing down what you say. I've been writing down all these notes since you were a baby.'
>
> 'Why?' she said, looking faintly shocked.
>
> 'Because that's what Daddy does. He tries to understand how little children think. That's his job.'
>
> She laughed at that. Daddies stared at blank pieces of paper all day and then went for long walks, talking to themselves. That surely couldn't bring you to an understanding of *anything*.
>
> 'You know what?' she said, obligingly. 'When I were a little baby, it were very sunny'.
>
> (2008: 5)

Fernyhough closely observed his daughter and genuinely tried to imagine, from her reactions, what she was thinking.

Colwyn Trevarthen has studied infant–parent interactions for more than 40 years, and has taught us a great deal about babies' interactions with their parents and carers, including the 'musicality' that very young babies and parents demonstrate when interacting. Similarly Daniel Stern carried out research into the 'interpersonal world of the infant', in his book of the same name, over a similar period of time, and offers theories of development, based on his observations (2003). Sue Gerhardt has written a significant and popular book on young children and their emotional development, called *Why Love Matters: How Affection Shapes a Baby's Brain* (2004). Her book gives the latest findings from neuroscience in an accessible way.

There has been a great deal of research into infant development in recent years. If you are embarking on a study of a baby, other literature you may want to access are books or papers by Antonio Damasio, Berry Brazelton and Joshua Sparrow.

Issues to consider

- What are the power issues involved when carrying out research with children and families, and how can I minimise the power differential?
- What might be the long-term effect of studying this child? How will they feel when they can read about themselves?
- How can I ensure that I behave ethically?
- How can I be sure I am not intruding?
- What about safeguarding? How can I communicate my responsibility to the parents of the child I am studying?
- Who owns the data, and who decides what should be included in any assignment or final report?
- How will I feed back what I consider to be 'poor practice' and to whom?

Additional information: gaining informed consent

If you are observing a child in a setting you must gain consent from all parents whose children attend, just in case they are caught on camera, although they would not be the main focus of your study. Many settings ask for this kind

Name of organisation or setting
Name of researcher ....

Dear Parents

I am undertaking a course on how children develop and learn: [name of course]
My report and short video will be shared with tutors on the course and an external examiner

I will be carrying out a study in your child's setting: [name of setting]
The duration of the study is from [date] to [date]
Your child may be caught on camera

My study will be written up by .... [date] and will be available for you to read

I will inform you if your child appears on film and invite you to view the film
....

Please let me know that you are willing for your child to be on film by signing below:

Signature of parent ....
Name in block capitals ....

Figure 2.1 Permission to film a group of children

of 'blanket permission' at the outset and then go back to the parents for any specific permissions to share the footage or photos more widely. If that is not done routinely, you might use something like the wording shown in Figure 2.1.

Permission to study a child for an observational study could be worded as shown in Figure 2.2.

Permission to study a child for an observational study could be worded like this:

Name of organisation

Dear .... [first names of parents]

I am currently undertaking a course on .... at
.... University. I am interested in carrying out a short study
of ....'s [child's name] play. The study will involve taking notes,
photos and film when s/he is absorbed in play at ....
nursery.

I am interested in ....'s play because...................................

I would very much like you to be involved in sharing with me how...................
plays at home and in helping me to understand ....'s play at
nursery. The material will be shared with my tutors and an external examiner.

If you are willing for ....to take part in the study, please sign
and return the slip below.

I will also be asking ....'s permission each time I observe him/her.
....

We are willing for .... to be involved in your study

Signatures of parents ....

Names in block capitals ....

Your sincerely .... [name of researcher]

Figure 2.2 Permission to film an individual child

3 Ways of gathering and recording data

Closely observing young children

[O]bserving is always subjective, but it can also be done with **rigour**. The rigour comes from observing and recording **in some detail** near, in time, to the event you are describing, and in a way that **initial judgements are not made**, and also from giving the **child's exact age** in each observation, so that progress can be clearly identified by the reader.

(Arnold, in Chapter 1 of this book)

I want to reiterate the idea that being subjective does not mean using anecdotes as evidence. Anecdotes are the kinds of stories we tell each other from memory, defined by the dictionary as 'a short account of an entertaining or interesting incident' (Tulloch, 1993: 51). What happens in these cases is that the story changes or becomes more sensational, for, as we recount the story, we reconstruct our memory of the original event. These stories are part of our lives and of how we interact with one another, but they do not constitute research.

Introduction

This chapter discusses:

- narrative observations
- children's drawings, models, etc.
- techniques for gathering data

- tools that can be used, including pen and paper, dictaphone, cameras, camcorders and smartphones, and including the advantages and disadvantages of each
- how we ensure we gather enough data.

Making narrative observations

Historically, paper and pen were the only simple way of preserving information to be shared and of capturing a moment in time. Although photography had been invented in the eighteenth century, cameras were not widely used and often only on special occasions. The quality meant that pen and paper could give the most accurate description in words of what was happening. Piaget made the sort of detailed observations of his children that his training as a biologist had required. The person I have tried to emulate when making narrative observations is Susan Isaacs, who ran an experimental school in Cambridge, England, in the 1920s. She described the method as follows: 'the records themselves are direct and dispassionate observations, recorded as fully as possible under the conditions; and as free as possible from evaluations and interpretations. Ideally, *no* interpretations should appear in the records' (1930: 1).

Isaacs wanted the reader to be able to interpret the meaning for himself or herself so she kept the observations and interpretations separate. She went on to say how the records were gathered:

> The observations (1924–7) offered here are taken from records written down by the educational staff in notebooks constantly carried about, at moments snatched from doing things actively with the children. We noted things as fully as we could at the actual moment and then dictated a fuller record from these notes, on the same day.
>
> (1930: 1–2)

This is not terribly different to the experiences I have had in nursery, keeping a kind of running record of the children's actions and speech. I strongly believe that children's speech must be noted word for word at the time, as remembering the exact words is difficult and, if we are considering development and learning, tiny changes can be noticed only if our records are accurate. Part of Isaacs' record in *Intellectual Growth in Young Children* is organised into four sample weeks. She was trying to give a sense of 'something approximating to the total behaviour' (Isaacs, 1933: 3). Here is an excerpt from the second week:

> Ages of children (in years and months): Frank (6;3), Tommy (3;11), Christopher (5;4), Priscilla (6;5), Dan (4;8), Phineas (2;11), Jessica (3;3), Conrad (5;0), Lena (3;1)

Phineas came with his mother, his second trial visit. He was very cheerful, and the others very friendly to him. He played ball with Jessica, Tommy and Christopher, who were very considerate and gentle. Yesterday he had burnt his mouth with hot cocoa, and so would not have any today. Later he played in the garden with the others, leaving his mother in the schoolroom quite cheerfully. Frank was making 'a path' through his garden plot, with barrowfuls of sand. He has carried this on for several days. Later on, he and Priscilla were swinging, and both tumbled out of the swing, scratching their hands a little. They asked for bandages, which were put on, and this led to a 'hospital' play. Both said they 'couldn't walk', and lay down on the rugs. The other children became 'nurses' and 'doctors', bringing medicine and water and so on. This hospital play carried on very freely and dramatically for a long time.

(1930: 225)

I could be critical and argue that adjectives like 'cheerful, friendly, considerate and gentle' are evaluations of behaviour, but what I gained from reading this account are some important points about the practice and what the children were interested in. Phineas at 2;11 was obviously being settled in by his mother, which would be considered good or wise practice nowadays, but was almost unheard of even in the 1970s when my children went to nursery. The settling-in was going well, as demonstrated by the fact that he allowed his mother to stay in the schoolroom while he went outside. There was an understanding about why he did not want cocoa, having burned his mouth the previous day. These observations tell me that Phineas's emotions were taken into account in this environment.

Carrying barrowfuls of sand for several days suggests to me that Frank was enjoying 'transporting' or carrying things, experiencing the weight of the sand (Athey, 2007). Later on, falling off the swing prompted some symbolic behaviour as doctors and nurses. Again, things were 'transported' to the patients.

The mix of ages meant that children could take on different roles, with the older children leading the play and learning, and the younger children participating in social scripts that may have been familiar to them.

Some guidance from *Understanding Children's Play*, first published in 1952

Hartley, Frank and Goldenson (1952: 341) draw on a previous work, *Child Psychology* by L.J. Stone, to give some guidance on the recording of behaviour. They say that, 'Running records are at once the most difficult and the most valuable records you will make. Here it is your task to record so fully, so thoroughly, and so vividly that you *reconstruct* the scene you have observed.' Below, I draw from their longer example, giving three versions of a short observation, each more detailed than the last.

Version One

'Johnny has been riding a tricycle with two other children since rest-time.'

(1952: 342)

Version Two

'Johnny has been riding a tricycle with two other children since rest-time. *He constantly glances around him as he rides, and hunches his shoulder as he approaches other bikes.*'

(1952: 342)

Version Three

'Johnny has been riding a tricycle with two other children since rest-time, *tramping the pedals in his characteristic, superenergetic fashion, emphasising energy rather than precision and often missing a pedal for a half-turn.* He constantly glances around him *challengingly (as though expecting interference?)* as he rides, and hunches his shoulder *(protectively?)* as he approaches other bikes.'

(1952: 343)

The authors, unlike Isaacs, emphasise that it is also important to 'add your *impression* and *interpretation* of the behaviour' as they have begun to do in brackets above, but also to extend this account close to the event. This can form part of your data. They also suggest practical aspects like having 'a prepared notebook' and using 'abbreviations and symbols for common words', all of which help keep your attention on observing (1952: 344).

A narrative observation of Georgia

> We (the maternal grandparents) looked after Georgia (aged 3y 8m 22d) while Colette was at work tonight. Georgia spent quite a while playing with Mahjong (which is a game which originated in China consisting of 144 tiles based on Chinese characters and symbols) – making patterns, matching tiles, infilling the box (so the tiles fitted in) and counting the symbols on the tiles. When she wanted to go on the computer, Pop (Grandad) told her she needed to pick up the tiles (that were all over the living room floor). She spent quite a while doing this. When she was counting the number of symbols on each tile (each tile had a small number in the corner like playing cards), she would say '8' immediately, but '7' she kept counting to check.
>
> (I sketched in the diary what the tiles looked like.)

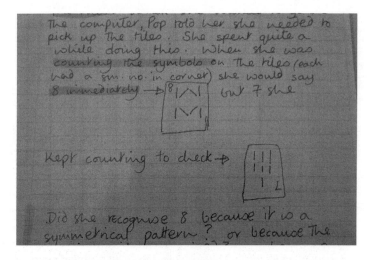

Figure 3.1 Diary showing a sketch of the tiles

Did she recognise '8' because it is a symmetrical pattern? Or because the number is easily recognised? Or because the number and pattern look the same either way up? Or because it looks very different to all of the other patterns?

(My notes recorded at the time)

As you can see, my observations are not as detailed as those recommended by Hartley *et al.*, but, using a sort of diary method, I do speculate immediately about why Georgia was recognising '8' on sight but seemed not to recognise '7' as easily.

As this was a longitudinal study (18 months plus) these initial speculations could be considered in the light of other actions recorded over time.

Figure 3.2 A mah-jong tile with the number in the centre

Different styles of writing

Different writers/researchers adopt different styles of writing about children. As we have seen, Isaacs was trying to give information about what happened without interpretation initially. Hall (1998) and Fernyhough (2008) are fathers, who are both authors, writing about their observations of their own daughters and they make a number of speculations about what might be happening and what might be the child's perspective on their world. All of this is integrated into their lively and fluent accounts. Fernyhough is also a lecturer in psychology, so he is able to integrate some of the latest theory from neuroscience into his account. They focus less on giving exact ages or reproducing observations word for word. One also gets the sense that they are writing something their daughters will read later on.

This brings me to the style adopted in many Learning Stories from New Zealand, in which the observer addresses the child. Learning Stories are an approach to assessment that documents children's learning in a family-friendly format, including the voices of child, parent and worker. Here is an excerpt from one example:

Building a Sticky Bridge

Written by Jacqui – 25th November

Today you and Lucy were very busy working in the collage area. You had the great idea of making a bridge with cellotape and were working with tremendous concentration to put this plan into action. Your bridge began to look like one of the pictures I had seen in my new bridge book, so I brought it to show you. You guys are great engineers!

(Carr and Lee, 2012: 60)

The observation is accompanied by a set of four photos and thoughts about 'the learning, further opportunities and a parent response', so is succinct but fairly comprehensive. The authors are clear that, when we make observations, we are 'constructing learner identities'. We are also opening events up for discussion with family and with the children themselves, thereby deepening everyone's understanding of the learning.

Children's drawings, models, etc.

Other important data to be gathered are the marks made by children and their other creations. If your focus is primarily on mark making, then you might want to gather everything a child produces over a period of time, which could be anything from a few weeks to a number of years (Hayward, 2012). If you are looking out for changes in behaviour, you might gather samples over the period of the study to be considered along with your observations. I would emphasise that much can be learned from observing the process of making marks. The actual product is often not of great importance to the child. What seems much more important is what they say and their body language while engaging in drawing. Again, asking 'What is it?' can be meaningless to a child as, often, they do not know. They may say something in response purely because they are being asked and children soon learn to respond to adults in predictable ways, which can be a great pity as it may crush the creativity most of us would wish to foster.

Helga Eng studied her niece Margaret's drawing 'from the first to the eighth year' (1931: vii). Eng used a naturalistic method, as I have described with Isaacs and the other examples in this book. She says:

Margaret had no instruction in drawing, but every now and then a drawing was made in front of her, in the first two and three years quite frequently, later on seldom, in the last years, almost never. This was usually done only at her own wish, and the drawing generally represented an object which she had chosen. Nobody asked her to draw, or kept her at it, nor were her drawings corrected and her mistakes pointed out. Nor did anyone ask her about her drawings ...

(1931: 2)

In the first part of her book, Eng presents examples of Margaret's drawings in chronological order. Eng gives Margaret's exact age in years, months and days as shown below, i.e. 1year, 10months, 20days. She uses descriptions in words, as well as Margaret's own spontaneous language and examples of the actual drawings. Here is an example of her description:

> At 1; 10, 20, she drew, as she had already been doing for the last two or three weeks on occasion, circles with points in them, and called the points eyes; but there were not two eyes alone, but a great many. In the smaller circle, which no doubt represents the head, a considerable number of 'eyes' are placed; above this she put some strokes and said 'hair'. To the larger circle she then added a line sloping upwards and said 'that's a leg': another line: 'that's another leg'.
>
> (1931: 20)

Eng went on to discuss Margaret's understanding of 'twoness', coming to the conclusion that she could recognise certain pairs but could not generally apply twoness or number two to everything, which is why Eng deduced that the number of eyes drawn did not match the number of eyes on a human face.

Chris Athey (2007) in her study, alongside their parents, of 20 children's schemas or repeated patterns at the ages of 2, 3 and 4, included written observations of the children's actions and their drawings in her account. Athey both appreciated and was critical of Eng's study. She appreciated the 'meticulously recorded background information' (2007: 66). However, Athey was critical that Eng gave most attention to 'content' at the expense of 'form' (2007: 66). Athey noted that, 'when Margaret draws "jagged teeth" Eng speculates on why she is feeling aggressive. She does not point out that "jagged teeth", "stairs" and many other types of content are drawn with a similar zig-zag form' (2007: 66).

While Eng was looking for differences and using a different theoretical framework to understand, Athey was searching for commonalities and was using a schematic framework to understand. Athey's study consisted of '5,333 observations' and '46% consisted of drawings, paintings and three-dimensional constructions'. So almost half of the data consisted of the children's creations. Athey goes on to say that, 'All observations were included in the analysis, except where several drawings were virtually identical' and given the same name by the child (2007: 62).

Athey was always looking for what children 'can do' and progress could be clearly illustrated in their drawings. Here is an example from a section on 'Separation and Connection':

> The following three drawings show a progression in the evolution of topological space notions. Lois (3: 1: 19) has started to *enclose* marks. The marks are *near* each other but *separated*. There is no *order*. Lois (3: 2: 10) draws a face *enclosure*. Hair is not yet *connected* to the head. The mouth (*horizontal scribble*) is *ordered* below nose and eyes. The *order* between the features shows an advance. *Horizontal* arms are

connected to the enclosure. Having drawn the two eyes with pupils for the first time, she held up her drawing and shouted out 'eye'. She then added the third 'eye' out of sheer ebullience.

(2007: 73–74; the *form* of schemas is printed in italics)

Although I am not able to reproduce the drawings here, you can see that the actual drawings would give an even clearer account of Lois's progress.

A more recent study focusing on children's creations is Kate Pahl's, entitled *Transformations: Children's Meaning Making in a Nursery* (1999). Pahl describes what she did:

> … through closely observing everything a group of children were hearing, doing and making when I observed a nursery class in a small inner city school for one term. I visited the classroom for two hours a week and recorded everything that happened in that period. I took away some of the models and drawings that the children created, or took photographs of what they produced …
>
> (Pahl, 1999: 10)

Pahl explained that she had 'a place in the classroom because my child was in the nursery', so she was seen as 'a parent who came and worked with them from time to time' (1999: 10). Pahl continued to work with individual children for a year and that data, plus things made at home and brought into the nursery, form part of the story.

I found this observation interesting:

The enabling space

Observation 13th September 1996

When I arrived the teacher had a big box and said he would be making things out of boxes. Lucy was making things out of straws. I sat at the drawing table and Abigail did a picture, made up of disassociated objects. One large one was her mummy (with a big tummy). Some children were playing with boxes. One child lay in a box during the entire session. When I went back to the drawing table some boys were drawing roughly: Jack drew a person, and Joseph drew a tree, a branch and a stone.

(Pahl, 1999: 41)

Following this, Pahl speculates that 'drawing is a way of being in something … a safe space', which made me think of 'withdrawing' (1999: 41). Through her observations, she began to see space as an expression. For example, Pahl recounts:

> Take my observation: that 'one child lay in a box during the entire session'. This child was using the box to express his need for safety.

Another child wanted things 'very small' – another meaningful state-ment. Space and size are important to children, whose body shape is changing as they move through the nursery experience.

(1999: 41)

You can see from this small excerpt of Pahl's account that she was observing as much as she could of what went on in that classroom, and trying to under-stand the children's thinking and feeling. Pahl noticed an important differ-ence between boys and girls in her study: 'While the girls tended to develop stories and then express their ideas in models … the boys would model in order to discover the story' (1999: 90).

This finding is not necessarily generalisable to all children as it comes from a comparatively small sample, but it does offer insights and things to look out for.

Georgia's creations

We gathered Georgia's creations at home and at nursery over a long period of time. Georgia made marks from early on, from which we saved samples. We documented how her writing began and developed. The painting shown here as Figure 3.3 was created when Georgia was 4y 5m 4d – notice that she has divided the paper, filled in just over half and written her name twice in the blank section. (For a set of photos showing this process, see the section below on using a camera to make observations.)

Figure 3.3 A painting

A salutary lesson from Harry about his thinking

When Harry was 5years 5months, he drew what is shown in Figure 3.4.

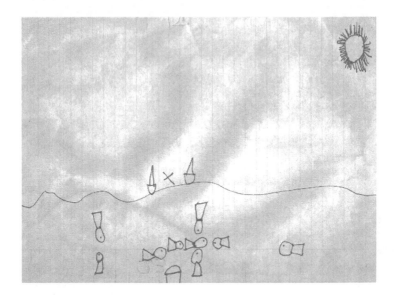

Figure 3.4 H's drawing at 5y 5m

When I put together Harry's story into the book *Observing Harry*, the editor and reviewers wanted me to arrange the observations in subject areas rather than chronologically through the book. I placed this illustration in the chapter on 'mathematical development' and named it 'fish in different positions'. I assumed a sunshine and two boats floating on the water. Many years later, when Harry was 17, I was checking out with him that it was OK for me to continue to use my observations of him in training for other early years workers and, specifically, the drawings. He and I were looking through them and discussing each one.

I asked, 'I wondered about the boats.'

Harry: 'They're not boats – they're dead fish, floating on the surface of the water. That's what they do when they're dead.'

I was surprised, to say the least, at this illumination of meaning after so long.

Harry added, 'I thought you would have known that – the cross means "dead"!'

This was a lesson to me in two ways – first, we can never make assumptions about what children are thinking and representing and, second, the power of that thinking, which had stayed with its creator after all of those years.

Techniques for gathering data

Some of the child studies carried out by parents attempt to capture as much data as possible and over a long period of time (Piaget, 1951; Matthews, 2003; Fernyhough, 2008). We see in those longitudinal studies that what is of significance is not always immediately apparent. It is often when one is able to make links with earlier observations that the child's intention becomes visible to others.

That is not possible if you are working with a child in a setting or visiting the family as a friend or relative. The techniques usually employed in gathering data involve either chunks of time spent observing the child or children, or observing specific events during the day or week. These two techniques are referred to as 'time sampling' and 'event sampling'.

Time sampling

Kate Pahl, discussed earlier in this chapter, referred to spending two hours in the setting once a week for a term and observing as much of what went on as possible. This was a sample of time from which she could extrapolate information about what the children did and made on a regular basis.

I have already mentioned the Tavistock Method, which involves a visit of one hour a week over a period of two years in order to understand a child's development from birth to 2. Again, this is a sample of time over a long period of study.

It is important to be systematic in your approach if you are carrying out an academic study. It is also vital to think through when you are most likely to gather the sorts of information you are seeking. In settings, the time of day can make a difference. If you want information on the variety of activities a child engages in, then you may want to visit or focus on that child at different times of day. If you are interested in transitions, you may want to visit or focus at transition times around arrivals and departures from the setting. Trying to be clear at the outset about when, for how long and how often you will observe a child is part of the systematic approach and this information should be underpinned by a rationale for the choices you have made.

Another approach that can be useful is to observe a child for one to two minutes at regular intervals, which could be every 15 minutes, every half an hour or even every hour (Webb, 1975: 70). This can be useful in gaining an overall impression of a child's actions over a morning or day, or, if used to observe several children, it can give a general impression of how children are interacting in the setting. This approach was used in the Effective Early Learning Project, led by Pascal and Bertram (1997). Staff in settings were trying to demonstrate that children were becoming more absorbed in play after engaging in the project, so very short observations of several children at regular pre-decided intervals gave that data.

A technique I have used as a first step in a long study was to track a child for a whole morning or afternoon, noting down what they did and said at one-minute intervals. I chose to do this in nursery in order to find out what their rhythm seemed to be. I used a prepared sheet (shown in Figure 3.5).

Name of child	Date ....
Event	Time
	9am
	9.01
	9.02
	9.03
	9.04
	9.05
	9.06
	9.07
	9.08
	9.09
	9.10
	9.11
	9.12
	9.13
	9.14
	9.15
	9.16
	9.17
	9.18
	9.19
	9.20
	9.21
	9.22
	9.23
	9.24
	9.25
	9.26
	11.00

Figure 3.5 Tracking sheet (two hours, minute by minute)

I had several questions in mind. I wondered whether they took a while to settle? How often they moved from one area to another? Whether they were able to access snacks? Who they interacted with? I then followed this up by observing them for 30 minutes once a week, during which time I took photos, gathered video and made notes. I was studying four children so this meant I dedicated a whole morning each week to observing each in turn (Arnold, 1997). This had implications for my colleagues, who needed to 'free me up' to gather data one whole morning a week.

Event sampling

An alternative approach is to watch out for when certain 'events' take place, which can be anything from 'initiating interactions with other children' to 'having a snack' and can result in understanding the extent or number of such events. In an early study I was involved in, when we were focusing on 'friendships', we decided to also watch out for 'conflict'. However, during the time span of the observations, we actually observed very little conflict.

This kind of approach can also be used to focus on a particular area of the setting, e.g. the block area, or on certain events during the day. Transition times can be particularly difficult for some children and a focus on understanding what is happening at those times, for example, during tidying up, can result in small action plans that make this time better for children and adults.

Podmore and Luff (2012: 35) suggest that, 'Teachers may also use event recording to monitor their own behaviour.' So making a note whenever you use 'negative or restrictive behaviour' can result in reflecting on, understanding and changing your own habitual behaviour. As a worker, it can be very useful to keep a journal and to reflect on your own behaviour afterwards in more detail. This would not be for sharing with others, but the act of writing and thinking about what happened and how you felt sometimes seems to bring about new awareness.

Tools and their advantages and disadvantages

Pen and paper

As described in the section on narrative observations, the main tool used to gather data for child observations over the years has been pen and paper. The focus has been on being physically able to write in enough detail for our notes to contain the essential information. Using abbreviated forms of some words helps. Also there are a number of schedules that have been developed in anticipation of the kinds of data we might gather. Figure 3.6 shows an example of a schedule for gathering information about a child's friendships.

The only danger in using a schedule is that other information might be ignored or missed altogether. If we are learning from children about children, how can we decide in advance what goes on to a schedule?

Name of child:	Date:
Observed by:	
For how long?	
How often the child interacted with adults	
How often the child interacted with other children How 'connected' their communication was	
Any conflict that occurred (Describe)	
Any other information relevant to developing friendships Shared humour? Shared pretend play?	

Figure 3.6 Schedule for observation

Schedules can be a useful way of reminding ourselves what we are looking out for, but they are limited and much more akin to large quantitative studies than to individual studies of children.

Another issue about using pen and paper is that writing takes up some of our attention, so we inevitably miss some of what children are doing when we write about what they are doing. Using the Tavistock model involves watching very carefully for an hour and then writing up in as much detail as possible afterwards what is remembered and how one felt.

Dictaphone

Using a dictaphone, or some other sound-recording device, ensures that an exact record of what is said is gathered. However, if you use only a dictaphone for your observations of children, a great deal of information is missed – for example, actions, body language and the rest of the context. Dictaphones can be useful as an additional tool if you want to record children's language when they are drawing, painting or engaging in role play.

Another use is for adults (either parents or workers) to talk through their observation, rather than writing them down. However, transcribing can be very time consuming, so I would only advise the use of a Dictaphone to listen back and to jot down important pieces of information.

Cameras

The use of photos to document children's learning has become very popular in settings. Photography is particularly useful to capture processes such as building with blocks. There was a time when most adults were looking for products as evidence of children's learning and when children were persuaded to 'draw something for mummy' that they were not really interested in doing. The use of photography enables workers to document *what children are interested in* that does not always result in an end product. A sequence of photos is more useful in communicating what happened than a single photo, but it takes quite a lot of skill and practice to capture the images. I find I take a lot more than needed and then pick out the ones that tell the story of what happened. Figure 3.7 shows four photos taken from a sequence of 16. Georgia is doing some painting and writing as shown in Figure 3.3.

Taking a sequence of stills from some video footage is much easier and more effective, but the quality is not as good.

Camcorders and smartphones

I find filming the most useful method of gathering observations, as the film can be viewed by the different people involved, including the child or children, and we can all contribute to the interpretation. There is something very vivid and immediate about watching a child on film. It is as though you were there in that moment.

However, there are disadvantages: like audio recording, the film has to be watched in real time, so that can be extremely time consuming. It is tempting and, in fact, essential to watch a film more than once as we frequently miss things during the first viewing. At the point of filming, only one person chooses where to point the camera, so other events in the environment can be missed. Also, the average camcorder picks up sound globally, resulting in less clarity when it comes to discerning language, especially if you are filming in a busy and noisy environment.

Figure 3.7 Georgia aged 4y 5m 4d, painting and writing

Being selective about what is filmed in the first place helps, as does categorising each clip so that they can easily be located again. A short child study over a few weeks may ask you to submit a five-minute film along with your written study. This can consist of five minutes of continuous filming or some shorter clips that link in some way, totalling five minutes. This takes practice and can rarely be achieved in one go, so be prepared to work at it. Basics like holding the camera still and having the light behind you help initially.

Some researchers, such as Trevarthen and Matthews, have developed more complex techniques, such as setting up three cameras to capture more of what is going on before synchronising the different versions into one film.

I find using a smartphone for photos and short filmed sequences very useful, as it is usually in my pocket and less intrusive than a camera. The child I am currently focusing on has just turned 2 but likes to look at herself on my phone. It is a way of her reflecting on her actions, and she usually responds to the bits she likes and watches them over and over again.

How we ensure we gather enough data

This is difficult to define as links need to be made between observations, and yet gathering huge amounts of data can be overwhelming. Most academic studies are defined by deadlines, so making a realistic plan about when, how and for how long you observe at the beginning does help. Even if you find yourself deviating from the plan, the chances are that you will gather enough data because you have thought the whole process through. Using video helps as you can look again and again at what you have filmed and see more. This gives your study depth, as your descriptions can be more detailed than is possible using other tools.

Building in time to gain permissions and to view the data alongside parents and other workers is another consideration.

Table 3.1 The advantages and disadvantages of the different tools used for documenting observations

Tool	Advantages	Disadvantages
Pen and paper	Easy to carry Unobtrusive	Takes our attention away from observing Time consuming
Dictaphone	Captures exact language used Unobtrusive Useful for adult to quickly record observations or immediate thoughts	Time consuming afterwards Misses actions and body language
Camera	Can capture process in a sequence of photos or final 'building'	Children may pose or become interested in using the camera Language missed
Camcorder or smartphone	A vivid account Can be viewed over and over again, and by different people	Does not capture whole context Can be intrusive Children might be affected by the camera Sound not so clear Time consuming – must be watched in real time several times When reading a transcript the meaning can get lost in the detail

Issues to consider

- What do I want to find out? (It helps to be clear about my questions.)
- How will I gather the data? (Often a mix of methods works best.)
- How often will I have access to this child/setting?

- When will be the best time of day to observe?
- How can I feed back to children, staff and parents?
- How can I involve parents and staff in interpreting the data?
- What does my overall plan look like?
- A useful checklist could be: How will I observe? When will I observe? What will trigger observations (e.g. the child's absorption in play)? How long will I observe for?

4   Making useful observations

> I think the core element for experiential education is that you take the experience of the other, of the learner, as a point of reference in whatever you do. So meaning that you try to sense, to feel, to understand how others make sense of the world.
>
> (Professor Ferre Laevers, 2014)

The purpose of carrying out a child study is usually to understand what the child is trying to learn about. So getting close and watching carefully can offer a huge amount of information. This chapter is concerned with ways of gathering the most useful information.

Introduction

This chapter discusses:

- identifying what we are trying to discover
- knowing when to focus on a child
- practising making observations
- getting some critical feedback
- ensuring that the observations fairly represent that child or children.

Identifying what we are trying to discover

When embarking on small studies, I have found it fairly easy to identify a main question and other questions that arise from the main question. For example, in the first small study I led on, I wanted to know whether children who play together are exploring the same schemas (Arnold, 1990). It was fairly obvious that we needed to observe the children playing together and identify what they were doing that was similar or different, in order to establish whether children are drawn to one another because they want to do similar things, or for some other reason. We found that: 'Children tended to play with other children, who were interested in doing similar things; clashes between children at nursery seemed to occur most often when children wanted the same toy; clashes between siblings at home occurred most often when children wanted to do different things' (Arnold, 1990: 32).

Referring back to Laevers' quote above, we very much wanted to understand how the study children were making sense of the world. That has been the aim in many child studies I have been involved in since.

It really helps to raise some questions that are of interest to you at the beginning of any process. The raising of questions can help you decide which tools/methods and techniques to use in order to find out.

In longer studies I have struggled more to define what I wanted to know about. It was not that I did not have questions, but I often struggled to communicate what they were. In my master's study, I had a very skilled tutor who helped me define what I was trying to discover. She encouraged me to **state those questions** right near the **beginning** and to return **to address** them towards **the end** of my study. This worked really well and is a technique anyone can use. Often our questions get lost during the process and then the reader gets lost too. These were my questions in a study of four children alongside their families, entitled *Understanding Young Children and Their Contexts for Learning and Development: Building on Early Experience* (Arnold, 1997):

- How can practitioners know what young children learn through the experiences nursery education provides?
- What role should the adults have in this learning?
- How do practitioners know where to start the process of extending children's learning and how do they find out?
- What are the most important points of reference between children, parents and practitioners? (By this I meant: What would be most helpful to notice and to talk about with parents?)
- How can these be used to inform teaching and learning processes in the nursery?
- What underpins the kind of practices that operate in one particular nursery centre (Pen Green), which can be used to inform other practices?

(Arnold, 1997: 3)

I am not suggesting these questions are perfect, but they worked for me at the time. I was actually really interested in knowing about children's home learning and how we could build on that at nursery, so maybe my questions should have been more focused on matching home and nursery experiences. For example, my questions might have been:

- How can we ensure that we build on children's home learning at nursery? (overarching or main question)
- How can we find out what are children's current and enduring interests?
- How can we plan to 'feed' those interests at nursery and assess what happens?
- What pedagogical approaches work most effectively?

Parent diaries

The parents kept a diary record of their child's actions and interests at home during the 18-month study, but the instructions I gave them on keeping the diaries were quite vague. However, in the introduction to the study I stated that I realised that the parents had the information I needed to gather:

> Firstly, we must ask the parents to share their knowledge of their own children with the practitioners. This presents a problem, however, as parents know so much about their own children that accessing the most useful knowledge may be difficult. One of the aims of this research project is to find better ways of sharing useful knowledge.
>
> (Arnold, 1997: 8)

The actual instructions given to parents, along with a diary, were to record anything 'curious or interesting' that their child did each week. This is what was written in the methodology section of the study:

> On-going parental field notes of child's home experiences and changes in family circumstances, structured only by providing a diary and fairly flexible instructions to observe what was 'curious' and 'interesting' and to note what the child spent most time doing at home along with an overview.
>
> (Arnold, 1997: 82)

By the time I wrote the conclusion, I realised that those instructions were not terribly helpful to the parents. This quote is from some of my notes that contributed to the conclusion:

> Parents need a much firmer structure for the observation of their children. 'Curious and interesting' is illuminating but limitless. A parent may not be able to take the high risk of writing anything. There may be a parallel in offering children limitless opportunities.
>
> (Arnold, notes)

Of the four families, one family (Georgia's) recorded events that made them laugh; another family used a dictaphone and recorded fairly mundane information, e.g. 'she watched TV' (their child was the youngest of the four study children and at nursery full-time, so exhausted when she got home); a third shared quite a bit about her child's emotional development and a fourth did not risk anything written at all, although she was a very able writer. I realised that the instructions I had given were poor. Also there was no comparable data across the four families. So, at this point, we needed to think about the parents' observations and how that could work better. What we really wanted were observations from parents that would help us plan for their child at nursery.

An observation from a parent diary

Here is an excerpt from the diary Georgia's parents kept. Much of the data they gathered consisted of conversations that revealed some of Georgia's preoccupations:

Georgia (aged 3y 8m): 'You are eleventeen?'

Mum: 'No'

Georgia: 'Six?'

Mum: 'No'

Georgia: 'Twenty?'

Mum: 'No I've been twenty'

Georgia: 'When were you twenty?'

Mum: 'Six years ago'

Georgia: 'That was one minute ago?'

Mum: 'No – six years ago'

Georgia: 'Six minutes ago?'

Mum: 'No – six years ago'

Georgia: 'Twenty years ago?'

Mum: 'No – six years ago'

This observation alerted the family and Georgia's workers to the fact that Georgia was interested in time passing and in understanding age in relation to time. **It offered a clue about what to look out for.** So other similar conversations were recorded that showed her emerging understanding.

When to observe

- How do you decide when to make observations?
- What is of most interest to you in children's play and actions?
- How could you engage parents in making observations at home?
- You may already be asking for contributions from families to children's records – if so how is that working? Do you use a diary or a blank sheet, or pose questions?

Knowing when it is a most useful and productive time to focus on a child

Observing children when they are deeply involved

It sounds really obvious now, but taking part in the Effective Early Learning Project, shortly after embarking on my master's study, provided a really steep learning curve for me (Pascal and Bertram, 1997). As a team, we were introduced to Ferre Laevers' research on 'involvement' as a concept (Laevers, 1997). This concept has been extremely useful in talking to parents about when to observe their children and make diary entries. The concept comes from earlier research by Csikzsentmihalyi, who studied adults' 'experience of playfulness'. He studied the whole phenomenon by interviewing groups of people, who spent a great deal of time and energy participating in activities with few or no 'extrinsic rewards'. These lengthy interviews produced very similar descriptions of 'how these people felt when the activity they were engaged in went well'.

> The first thing people mention is the issue of concentration or involvement which is described as a merging of action and aware-ness. You are not thinking about doing something, you are doing it, and while you're doing it you are not aware of alternatives, nor are you aware of certain other problems. There's a filtering out of irrel-evant stimuli which happens almost automatically.
>
> (cited in Sutton-Smith, 1979: 260)

There is a feeling of being completely absorbed: 'It's like flowing, it's like being carried away and yet being in control of the direction of the flow' (Sutton-Smith, 1979: 261). Laevers (1993: 55) linked 'the experiential attitude' of the teacher trying 'to get in touch with the process of experiencing in the child', with 'the provision of materials and activities' and 'moments when the teacher is involved in dialogue or sustains activity by giving stimulating impulses'. The teacher offers challenge to match capabilities. In other words, Laevers looked at utilising moments when development was most likely to be occurring.

He drew on Csikzsentmihalyi's ideas about the 'state of flow' as well as Piagetian ideas about recently acquired schemas.

Following my master's study and what we had learned from the Effective Early Learning Project and Laevers' research, we (the Pen Green Team) wasted no time in sharing with parents his idea of **'deep level learning' occurring when children are deeply involved or absorbed** (Laevers, 1997; Whalley, 2007). The concept is easily understood by everyone, and parents – as well as workers – are then able to be more discerning about what to note down or film. Being aware of 'involvement' as a concept also very quickly brings to our attention any children who are not becoming very involved some of the time.

Note that we would not expect very high involvement for the whole of a child's time at nursery, but highs and lows during a session are usual. Exploring new learning is exhausting, as we all know, so some 'time out' just to ponder is necessary to everyone. Also judging children's involvement is not so much a judgement of a child but of the provision we are offering them to match their interests. So consistently low involvement can alert practitioners to improve the resources and environment on offer to a child.

How does 'involvement' work for different children?

So would knowing about 'involvement' have helped in observing Georgia? My understanding of the concept of 'involvement' as explored by Laevers and his team is that the involvement scale and signals lend themselves well to observing children who become very involved with objects or resources. **A word of caution here:** this has been my interpretation, well suited to Piaget's idea of a lone explorer. Laevers might see the concept differently. Georgia was not one of those children, who was a 'lone explorer'. I have discussed this with her recently and, even at 23 years of age and at work, she is aware that she 'never zones out people'. That was also the case when she was a young child. What was of most interest to her was what other people were doing, and the questions she asked were concerned with other people, their ages, what they were allowed to do, where they went, what size of friendship bracelet would fit them … to name but a few. I have thought for some time that the signs of involvement for children, who, like Georgia, zone in on people, might be slightly different or could be expanded.

However, the concept of 'involvement' worked really well for her brother, Harry, who would deeply investigate his burning interests over long periods (Arnold, 2003).

The involvement scale consists of statements describing 'low involvement or uninvolved' at level 1, up to 'very high involvement and not to be distracted' at level 5. Alongside the scale, the following 'signals' are articulated: 'concentration; energy; complexity and creativity; expression and posture; persistence; accuracy; reaction time; language; satisfaction' (Laevers, 1997: 18). For a child like Georgia, as I see it, the so-called 'distractions' provided much of the learning.

Building on the idea of involvement by identifying 'chuffedness'

During a Pen Green study of children's 'Well-being and Resilience', Colette Tait (2004, 2005) extended this idea of 'satisfaction' to include 'chuffedness' displayed by children occasionally when they were really pleased with themselves. Tait (2004) explains:

> We began to notice that some children were displaying what we are calling 'chuffedness' (Research dialogue with Trevarthen, 2002). They were showing that they were intrinsically pleased with themselves, *for themselves*. They were displaying chuffedness in very individual ways, but leaving us with no doubt that they were completely fulfilled. Some of the different ways in which we saw children being chuffed were:
>
> - Singing or 'crowing' with joy
> - Deep sighing, as though with complete satisfaction
> - Smiling
> - Gesturing for people to look at what they had done
> - Raising their arms as though to say 'look at me'
> - Swaggering
> - Putting their tongue in their cheek (as though pleased with themselves, and unable to hide their pleasure if they wanted to)
>
> (Tait, 2004: 6–7)

The Pen Green Team went on to investigate with one another, as adults, what needs to be in place for 'chuffedness' to occur, and found that 'choosing' what to do was important, as was 'a struggle', 'effort' or 'challenge', and finally some sort of 'mastery' (Tait, 2004: 8). So, if you see a child displaying 'chuffedness', that is always worth recording. It is also a good topic to discuss with parents as they will be aware of how their own children display that ultimate satisfaction with what they are doing. Tait followed up the subsequent year by considering 'Chuffedness as an Indicator of Quality in a Baby and Toddler Nest' (2005), so again these tools were used not only to judge when to observe and notice the children's satisfaction, but to improve the provision for children.

How other researchers have decided when to focus on children

Atherton and Nutbrown (2013: 25) describe spotting schemas in 'the day care setting of a Children's Centre' as follows: 'sitting waiting watching, listening, photographing and talking were the means by which, over time, incidences of similar patterns of behaviour were identified in the Children's Centre and at home'. **Useful observations** were made by 'waiting, watching', and recording and eventually making links between observations. This idea of identifying patterns in the children's play, but also in your data, is important.

Hayward (2012: 124) set up a mark-making table in a reception class and was available to have conversations with the children while they were engaging in mark making, knowing that this situation was likely to give her the data she was seeking. Although the provision was available to the class, her focus was on 'five children, who had previously attended the Pen Green Nursery ... whose parents and workers has reflected on their mark making at nursery' (2012: 124). **Useful observations** were made at a table specifically set up for what Hayward hoped to observe.

A practical issue is to have the tools to hand, if you intend focusing on something like a child's 'involvement'. So paper or notebook and pen, as Isaacs mentioned, should be carried around with you. Cameras and camcorders should be charged and available very near to where you are observing so that you can just pick them up and film or photograph at the optimum time.

Recording children's questions

Another source of information, which is helpful in identifying children's deep interests and learning is their questions, which can be anything from 'What's that?' to more complex hypotheses, depending on the age, development and experience of the child. Piaget became interested in the questions his own children asked spontaneously and then, later, in his clinical interviews with older children, he posed some of the same questions in order to establish a more generalised understanding of children's understanding of concepts. I would argue that there is a big difference between what children ask spontaneously, from which we can deduce their interest and understanding, and the questions we pose, as adults. Here are some examples of the spontaneous questions asked by his own children of their father Jean Piaget:

> ... L., at 3 ; 4 (3) ... she watched a cloud moving: *'Is the cloud an animal?'*
> (1951: 252)

> At 5 ; 7 (17) J., having asked three days earlier if clouds were made with cement, put the question in a new way: *'What are clouds made of? –* Do you know? *– Liquid –* that's right *– It's water, evaporated water'*
> (1951: 254)

> At 5 ; 7 (20) (J) *'Well how does it stay in the sky? Like balloons?'*
> (1951: 254)

(The child's words are in italics.)

Many of his children's questions were about air and wind, and how things move, and based on their experience of the world. One question that resonated with me was J's, asked 'at 3 ; 7 (12) seeing the sun rise in the mountains at an unexpected place: *'Are there two suns then?'* In one of my earlier studies, there was a similar example:

> Often we see Harry puzzled or not quite understanding the process of time passing and change. For example, Harry (aged 2years 8months)

expresses his idea that '*Uncle Paul has two cats*'. Harry has seen Jasper the kitten and Jasper the cat. Harry's parents explain that the kitten has grown up. They find it difficult to convince Harry that the kitten and cat are one and the same.

(Arnold, 2003: 28)

These sorts of puzzles presented to us by children offer a great deal of food for our thinking. Nathan Isaacs, in an appendix to *Intellectual Growth in Young Children*, discusses children's 'Why' questions, and explains that they arise because of 'a sudden clash, gap or disparity between our past experience and any present event' (Isaacs, 1930: 295). In other words, to use Piaget's term, children ask 'Why?' when they become disequilibrated just as Jacqueline and Harry did in the above examples. Their disequilibration, or confusion, gives us a clue about what they want to know about and their current understanding.

Jacqui Cousins, in her book *Listening to Four Year Olds*, describes an astute little boy who asks lots of questions:

Sonnyboy asked innumerable questions of his very patient teacher and had very strong beliefs about the nature of classroom questions. He lost his sunny smile when she asked questions which, to him, were not real questions which everyone had to puzzle over, but were questions to which the teacher and most of her pupils already knew the answer. In his words to his teacher: 'why do you keep asking us questions when you know all the answers? Like "What colour is it, then?" You can see for yourself it's red, so why do you keep asking?'

(1999: 16)

Although Sonnyboy's question seemed blunt, it was genuine. Cousins adds that questioning seems to be 'particularly intense at four' (1999: 22). Cousins recorded the children's conversations and, when they listened to her recording, even the children themselves were surprised at the frequency with which they asked questions. So, as a source of data in a child study, recording (in some way) children's spontaneous questions or asking their parents to keep a record of their questions, could be quite productive.

Practising making observations

In Podmore and Luff's book on observation (2012: 104), Sarah Te One reflects on making observations:

Having time to sit and watch children and adults go about their day-to-day play and work in a centre was a luxury. I remember the first day of observations – the clean notebook, the new document on the laptop and a sense of freedom, I suppose. I could observe what and how I wanted (within the bounds of the ethics agreement, of course). In a sense, it was overwhelming – where do I start? In the end, it began with who was in front of me, and I wrote and wrote and wrote some more.

She goes on to describe the act of observing and writing as 'a springboard for more ideas about what to look out for' (2012: 104). Sarah notes how very 'exhausting' the whole process was and that, 'Rather than the question of what to observe, at times it became a question of what not to observe' (2012: 104).

In the same text we hear the thoughts of Lesley Rameka, as a lecturer and a grandparent: 'The challenge for educators, I believe, is to capture the warmth, humour, and joy of children's learning. This requires that we do not stand back as cold, aloof, unbiased observers, but embroil ourselves enthusiastically in the process, celebrating the learning' (2012: 103).

She goes on to describe observation as 'seeing rather than looking' and 'akin to putting on a pair of glasses that allows you to see what was previously unnoticed' (2012: 103). So we are definitely looking to see more when we intentionally focus on observing a child or children.

If observing children is new to you, then you can learn how to do it only by doing it. It is experiential in a sense. It can help to read the observations of other writers to see what communicates well with you. I have tried to adopt the style of Susan Isaacs, as I believe she wrote in plain English what she saw happening, without judgement whenever possible. I can follow the story of what happened in the Malting House School from her records. When you write up a child study, think of it as **the story of what happened**.

You do need to practise, as making written observations in the moment or from video does not come naturally to most people. I have sometimes had to watch a video clip many times in order to pick up a child's language. As I have already stated, language is best recorded accurately at the time. There is no point in recording language that is inaccurate. Occasionally adults inadvertently 'correct' a child's language when they write it down. Again, this would not be acceptable for a study.

An example of a transcript of a filmed clip

Here is an example of a transcript of a three-minute clip filmed at nursery when Georgia was 3y 9m 2d:

> There are three children, two trailers and two climbing frames outside. G climbs over one trailer and goes around it and picks up the handle. Sam climbs into the trailer, saying to Lana (and pointing) 'You have that one.' G also points

towards the other trailer. Sam lies down in the first trailer. G pulls it around 90 degrees, then hesitates, looking towards the camera, before standing still, facing Sam and leaning the handle of the trailer on her hip ...

She pulls the trailer around the square climbing frame. Lana runs after them saying something about 'going out on the minibus.' Sam leans out of the back of the trailer and says 'I'm not going.' G circles around the square frame four times. The trailer gets caught on the frame on the third time and she pauses to unhook it before continuing. She starts to go around a fifth time. Sam points towards the gate and says something. G shakes her head. Sam climbs out of the trailer and onto the 'A' frame. G places the handle on the ground and goes towards the 'A' frame. Sam says something and points towards the gate again. G returns to the trailer, picks up the handle and walks quickly towards the gate, looking down at the trailer behind her as she walks. She loops the handle of the trailer over a post, which is about chin high, and is near the gate. Lana comes over and looks. G jumps and runs, saying 'I'll put yours on there as well!' She dashes back to the 'A' frame and pulls Lana's trailer to the post, then struggles to hook the handle over.

(A slightly longer version of this observation is used in Chapter 7 for the purpose of deeper analysis.)

At the time I analysed this clip using the AIRSS framework (see below), which developed during the project as the points of reference seemed to keep cropping up.

- **Autonomy:** G displayed autonomy by acting spontaneously when she picked up the handle of the trailer, led the way around the frame and stopped to unhook the trailer when it got caught. She shook her head at one of Sam's suggestions and expressed what she clearly wanted to do when she offered to hook Lana's trailer on the post.
- **Involvement:** G was involved throughout, but was most motivated when walking quickly to the post, and dashing to repeat her action with Lana's trailer.
- **Relationships:** G clearly had relationships with Sam and Lana, but there seemed to be a sort of pecking order. Sam seemed to be in charge, so G listened to her and looked towards her for signals. Lana followed the other two children and seemed agreeable to G hooking her trailer on the post.

- **Schemas:** G was using *trajectory, transporting, enclosure* and *connection* schemas during this clip. She *transported* Sam, mostly making an *enclosure* with the route she chose. When something became more pressing (or important to her) she walked quickly in a *trajectory* towards the gate. She coordinated a *trajectory* (the post) with an *enclosure* (the handle) and *connected* the trailer to the post by placing the handle over the post. She chose to be *connected* to Sam, showing the emotional link between the children.
- **Strategies:** G's main strategy was action. She also showed her allegiance to Sam when she pointed towards the second trailer, indicating that Lana should have that one.

Getting some critical feedback

Although it may seem a little intimidating at first, the best way to improve your practice and writing is to share it with others and to ask for honest critical feedback. If you are on a course, it helps to have a 'study buddy', who could be one of your fellow participants on the course. You may also have colleagues at work or family members who would willingly read your observations and give you feedback about how well you are communicating.

A critique of my observation

I could quite easily critique several points in my own observation above, as follows.

1 The actual observation does not communicate much in the way of emotion.
2 I say in the analysis that 'Georgia displayed autonomy', but there is nothing in my written description to indicate that display. Perhaps I could have said something like 'Georgia quickly took the initiative and ...'
3 Using the written observation as reference, the reader would not have known when Georgia was most involved. I needed to say something like 'Georgia displayed most energy when she walked towards ...'
4 The 'pecking order' could have been made more explicit by drawing attention to facial expressions, when the children were interacting.

Someone, who has not been involved, can ask useful questions that help clarify your meaning.

Approaching the task of observing

- Whose observations do you admire?
- What sorts of data would you like to gather?
- How will you go about making your observations?
- How can you see things afresh?

Ensuring that the observations fairly represent that child or children

Your closest allies in making sure that you are representing the child or children you study authentically and fairly are the parents and/or carers. Whatever you observe can be explained and supplemented by the information the family holds. As workers, we share only a little of children's lives. Also we need to be clear about what are our interests and what are the child's or children's interests. The ongoing dialogue with parents/carers and also colleagues or your study buddy can help you question any 'taken for granted' assumptions that you make initially.

If you are a parent studying your own child, it is still essential to dialogue about your observations with your partner, a relative or friend. That is often when the learning becomes visible.

Issues to consider

- What questions do I have?
- How can I engage the parents/carers in observing their child and sharing information with me?
- Would it help to record this child's questions? That might be something the parents could do as well.
- Do I have a 'study buddy' to share my observations with?
- Are my descriptions detailed enough to reconstruct the scene and for the reader to be able to interpret?

5 Selecting material to include in a child observation study

> Every now and then go away, have a little relaxation, for when you come back to your work your judgment will be surer. Go some distance away because then the work appears smaller and more of it can be taken in at a glance and a lack of harmony and proportion is more readily seen.
>
> (Leonardo da Vinci)

This famous quote by Leonardo da Vinci is relevant to child study in the sense that collecting data, becoming overwhelmed by it and then stepping away can give you a clearer perspective on the learning. You also need to be able to view all of your data in order to gain a balanced sense of the learning over the period of study.

Introduction

This chapter discusses:

- how to interact with the data and reduce it to a manageable amount to include in the final written study, including …
- reducing your data to an appropriate length
- ways to highlight significant events
- viewing the whole data set (all of the observations at once).

How to interact with the data

When you have made your observations and gathered your data, you probably will have:

- some written narrative observations
- some filmed material

- photos, including sequences of photos
- children's creations
- information from parents
- reflections on the learning from your journal.

Integrating all of this information into a coherent story is the next task. **Putting everything into a chronological order** is the first step in that process. The data can feel unmanageable unless you are able to reduce it and see it as a whole. What sometimes happens is that not all of the data is considered. I sometimes see observations put into an appendix that are actually more illuminating than the information that has been included in the study. Blaxter, Hughes and Tight (1996: 177) suggest that you need to 'Think about by how much you will need to reduce the volume of your data in order to present, analyse and discuss it, within the space you will have available.'

Qualitative data takes up a lot more space than quantitative data and, in some ways, is harder to handle. So how do you choose what to include? Roberts-Holmes (2005: 157) emphasises that 'Knowing the literature in your topic area will greatly assist you with the process of identifying the significant data you have collected.' So, familiarity with the literature on development and learning, and any aspect of learning you are particularly interested in, should help when deciding what to include. The literature may also help you decide how you want to explore the topic, as in the following example.

Georgia's Story

When I embarked on writing *Georgia's Story* I had read most of the literature available at that time on schemas. I had read Athey's *Extending Thought in Young Children: A Parent–Teacher Partnership*, which I found totally inspirational in terms of understanding schematic theory and how young children 2–5 years explore schemas. What I missed was being able to track one child's story chronologically. This experience influenced the study and book I wrote subsequently. I decided to follow four children over 18 months alongside their parents. The study is presented as four separate stories, and one of the foci is schemas (Arnold, 1997). *Georgia's Story* is one child's story, including the schemas explored and concepts being developed, so that readers can see how Georgia's learning developed over time (Arnold, 1999). Athey emphasised the universal nature of schemas by presenting data on or examples of 20 children exploring schemas throughout her book. I emphasised the uniqueness and continuity of each child's explorations by focusing on each child in turn. I have taken a similar approach to other studies – for example, *Understanding Schemas and Emotion in Early Childhood*, which is made up of seven short studies of children (Arnold and the Pen Green Team, 2010).

How to reduce your data to an appropriate length

Returning to the issue of reducing the information to a manageable length to present, Blaxter *et al.* (1996: 184) make an important distinction: 'Are you summarising or choosing certain bits of data to emphasise and discuss?' Either approach could work. I have always been keen to offer direct quotes of observations of what children and their parents say, so I would say I am inclined to select certain bits of data to provide evidence to support what I am saying. Roberts-Holmes (2005: 157) supports this idea in saying that 'choosing data is often to do with the construction of an argument or idea which you believe in and wish your study to highlight'.

So, to sum up, you reduce the data to a manageable length either by:

- summarising the whole story, or
- by choosing certain bits of data that link or that you want to emphasise.

Example of raw data

Georgia (aged 2y 5m 18d) at Mop's house at 5pm

There were lots of bits of paper on the couch when I got home. Georgia was carrying a clutch bag. It contained 'tickets' and real money. She ran to the couch to get a picture for me and made a mark on it. As she made the mark she said 'Write Mop'. She then gave me all of the tickets and talked about 'Paying'. She gave me some money and expected me to give her some back. She gave me all of the copper coins and she kept the silver ones. She referred to the 20p as a 'Choo choo', which is a ride on a toy train at the supermarket. I said I would be paying for my game of golf the next day. She said 'Pay golf?' a couple of times. She pretended to count the money.

A **summary** of the above observation, to be included along with summaries of other observations, might look like this:

> Georgia (aged 2y 5m 18d) played with bits of paper and money. The paper represented tickets and she pretended to count and to write. She was exploring the meaning of 'paying'.

Choosing data to include might look like this:

> Georgia (aged 2y 5m 18d) was 'carrying a bag' containing 'tickets' and 'money'.
>
> She 'made a mark on paper and said 'Write Mop'.
>
> She explored 'paying' by giving me some money 'but expected me to give her some back' and queried 'Pay golf?'
>
> Georgia seemed to have some sense of the value as 'she gave me the copper coins and she kept the silver ones'.
>
> 'Choo choo' is her symbolic name for 20p.
>
> 'Pay golf?' seemed to surprise Georgia.

Ways to highlight significant events in your data

So once you have put everything into a chronological order, you need to **read through it all several times** and/or view video and listen to any sound recordings so that the whole dataset is familiar to you. Use a pen or highlighter to **mark words or phrases that seem significant** to you – for example, what you want to make sure to include in a summary or what you may want to quote in a final account. This is a subjective process and based on what you, personally, find interesting or intriguing. It may be to do with a child's understanding – for example, 'Pay golf?' repeated suggests that this is a new idea to Georgia, so would seem significant in some ways. Blaxter *et al.* (1996: 184) offer some guidance about possible ways of interacting with your data at this point:

> *'Coding'* – 'The process by which items or groups of data are assigned codes'. This helps you to look for similarities in the data and to pull all of those similar pieces together'.

Applying *coding* to the above observation might look like this:

> 'There were **lots of bits** (*quantity*) of paper on the couch when I got home. Georgia was carrying a clutch bag. It contained "tickets"

and real money. She ran to the couch to get a picture for me and made a mark on it. As she made the mark she said "Write Mop". She then gave me **all of the tickets** (*quantity*) and talked about "Paying". She gave me some money and expected me to give her some back. She gave me **all of the copper coins** (*quantity*) and she kept the silver ones. She referred to the 20p as a "Choo choo", which is a ride on a toy train at the supermarket. I said I would be paying for my game of golf the next day. She said "Pay golf?" a couple of times. She pretended to **count** (*quantity*) the money'.

(In this instance I have only applied one code 'quantity'. I chose this because it cropped up a few times and I thought Georgia was possibly exploring quantity. An action in this short observation that crops up more than once is 'giving' so I might mark that as a second code to watch out for in subsequent observations.)

'Annotating' – 'This is the process of adding or making notes or comments. I have found this really useful when watching video as an ongoing record of how my own ideas about the learning are developing. This opens things up and may guide what else to look out for'.

(Blaxter *et al.*, 1996: 184)

Applying *annotating* to the above observation might look like this:

(My annotated comments are in square brackets and in italics.)

There were lots of bits of paper on the couch when I got home. Georgia was carrying a clutch bag. It contained 'tickets' and real money. She ran to the couch to get a picture for me and made a mark on it. As she made the mark she said 'Write Mop'. *[Is she understanding that when a mark is made, it means something? Writing her name on paper might be familiar. Is she applying that to me?]* She then gave me all of the tickets and talked about 'Paying'. She gave me some money and expected me to give her some back. *[What is Georgia's understanding of paying? Does she see money exchange hands at the shops? How can I help her understand about values of different coins?]* She gave me all of the copper coins and she kept the silver ones. *[She has a rough idea that silver is better to hold on to than copper.]* She referred to the 20p as a 'Choo choo', which is a ride on a toy train at the super-market. *[She has created her own symbolic name, based on what can be bought for 20p, i.e. a ride – does she do this with any other coins?]* I said I would be paying for my game of golf the next day. She said 'Pay golf?' a couple of times. *[She seems surprised I have to pay for golf – is that outside of her experience?]* She pretended to count the money.

'Labelling' – 'This can be useful when you already have an idea about the analytical frameworks you will use – for example, you might high-light or underline in your written data "repeated actions" or "schemas" in order to locate them easily again'.

(Blaxter *et al.*, 1996: 184)

Applying *labelling* to the above observation might look like this:

(I had decided to look for evidence of possible 'repeated patterns of action' or 'schemas', and had looked at the list in Chapter 6 of this book, so wanted to label any possible schemas in order to see if Georgia repeated the actions on other occasions. I have underlined words and phrases that give me clues about possible schemas, and have added the schema name in brackets after the word or phrase or at the end of the sentence.)

There were lots of bits of paper on the couch when I got home. Georgia was <u>carrying</u> (transporting?) a clutch bag. It <u>contained</u> 'tickets' and real money (containing?). She ran to the couch to get a picture for me and made a mark on it. As she made the mark she said 'Write Mop'. She then <u>gave me</u> all of the tickets (transporting?) and talked about 'Paying'. She <u>gave me</u> some money and expected me to give her some back (transporting?). She gave me all of the copper coins and she kept the silver ones (transporting?). She referred to the <u>20p as a 'Choo choo'</u>, which is a ride on a toy train at the supermarket (transporting? 20p represents the ride symbolically). I said I would be paying for my game of golf the next day. She said 'Pay golf?' a couple of times. She pretended to count the money.

'Selection' – 'This is used when selecting certain passages or stories or instances to illustrate what you are finding out. Be wary of what is being omitted if you use this approach. There is always the danger of missing out information that does not fit with what you think is the case and, therefore, not being open to new information that the data is offering you'.

(Blaxter *et al.*, 1996: 184)

Applying *selecting* to the above observation might look like this:

There were lots of bits of paper on the couch when I got home. <u>Georgia was carrying a clutch bag. It contained 'tickets' and real money.</u> She ran to the couch to get a picture for me and made a mark on it. As she made the mark she said 'Write Mop'. She then <u>gave me all of the tickets and talked about 'Paying'.</u> She gave me some money and expected me to give her some back. <u>She gave me all of the copper coins and she kept the silver ones.</u> She referred to the 20p as a 'Choo choo', which is a ride on a toy train at the supermarket. I said <u>I would</u>

be paying for my game of golf the next day. She said 'Pay golf?' a couple of times. She pretended to count the money.

(The underlined parts are what I might want to quote and focus on discussing in my final account as Georgia seems to be intrigued by money, how it is used and in what circumstances.)

'*Summary*' – 'This involves summarizing what has happened'.

(Blaxter *et al.*, 1996: 184)

Applying *summarising* to the above observation might look like this:

Georgia (aged 2y 5m 18d) experimented with quantity by manipulating tickets and money and moving them around. Some of her play was symbolic.

(You will notice that this summary is different to the earlier one, even though I was summarising the same observation. This is a subjective process, so any two people might see things differently. That is one reason why it is a good idea to discuss the observations with the child's parents and with colleagues so you gain the view of those people most familiar with the child's play and explorations.)

These are all slightly different processes and you may want to try using more than one way of interacting with your data to see what becomes apparent or visible. Miles and Huberman (1994: 58) point out that 'codes can be at different levels of analysis, ranging from the descriptive to the inferential', and they help to 'group disparate pieces into a more inclusive and meaningful whole'.

For example, an initial code used above was 'quantity', which denoted any link to 'amount' in Georgia's play. Later on in the process, this coding became more refined. At 3y 10m Georgia began to 'estimate', which provided a more accurate label for her actions and thinking in the data. At 3y 11m Georgia became interested in 'limits' and in what is 'finite' and what is 'infinite'. She asked about the computer 'Will the G's run out?' At this stage of coding, we were inferring from her questions what she was exploring. In this way, the coding moved from being quite general and descriptive, i.e. 'quantity', to being inferential, i.e. her question about the computer 'Will the G's run out?' suggested that she was interested in 'limits'.

They also suggest that 'a start list of codes can be created prior to the fieldwork' based on questions raised or conceptual frameworks being considered. What does not fit, sometimes referred to as 'rogue data', is as important to include, as that which seems to fit. The so-called 'rogue data' may help raise unanticipated questions. For example, at 2y 5m 11d Georgia 'Likes saying "Walter" and repeats the name several times.' This observation did not seem to link with other observations and made us wonder 'Does she just like the sound of the name?' or 'Is Walter a person whose name she has heard?'

Georgia was always very interested in other people, so it may have been that she heard the name on TV or in passing and she liked the sound of it. It was unusual to her perhaps. Much later on Georgia would repeat words or phrases she liked the sound of or was intrigued by – for example, at 3:9:4 Georgia talked about 'a barrowful of apples', 'a frog in my throat' and 'ants in my pants'; at 3:9:11 she said that her friends were 'desperate' to see her new shirt. So we began to see links through language that fascinated Georgia.

Viewing the whole dataset

I enjoy gathering data, so each of my studies has generated a huge amount of it. In my master's study this consisted of: thousands of words of written observations; filmed material; photos including sequences of photos; parent diaries; video from home; and a journal of incidental information and reflections (Arnold, 1997). The journal alone consisted of 30,000 words.

Miles and Huberman (1994: 141) state that, 'Analysis of qualitative data rests very centrally on displays that compress and order data to permit drawing coherent conclusions, while guarding against the overload and potential for bias that appears when we try to analyse extended, unreduced text.'

They go on to suggest that, 'Two major families of displays are matrices (rows by columns) and networks (nodes connected by links).' These can be used to 'build a display' of your data. (See Tables 5.1 and 5.2 for examples of matrices.)

I was at a point in my master's study when I was feeling overwhelmed and not sure how to handle the amount of data I had gathered, when I came across Andrew Pollard's longitudinal study of children's social worlds of learning. Pollard studied ten children in a primary school. He was interested in the *Social World of Children's Learning*. He states that he wanted to understand the 'social factors in play' in relation to children in schools (Pollard with Filer, 1996: xi). He further explains, 'I particularly focused on the social factors which were likely to influence the children's stance, perspectives and strategies regarding learning' (1996: xii). He collected a huge amount of data from parents, peers, teachers and the headteacher. He made observations in the classrooms and recorded discussions with the children, as well as gathering documentation. Pollard admits that 'A brief attempt to develop a coding scheme to classify each small element of data quickly proved itself to be both mechanistic and impractical, and there was a period during which I feared that the volume of data could prove unmanageable' (1996: 298).

Pollard found that he needed a **way to reduce the data** so he could see an overview of each child's learning each year and, from the overview, he constructed the case studies, which were of individual children.

Although I had read about these matrices in the research literature, it was only when I saw what Pollard had done that I realised that the same system of reducing the data to a table (or matrix) might also work in my study. It was a case of reducing a large amount of qualitative data to words

Table 5.1 How data can be reduced and viewed as a whole before expanding into a coherent story

---

AIRSS analysis - Oct–Dec 1994 (Georgia aged 3y 8m to 3y 11m)

Autonomy - confidence on computer; own design; seek comfort; choose toys to take; spontaneous decoration of Xmas tree; choose role; saying "No"; starting game
Involvement - fastening; on computer; stories; planning; painting; chasing game
Relationships - maternal grandparents; mum; dad; Harry; Samantha: Stephanie; Laura; Craig
Schemas - enclosure; transporting; core and radial; connection; fit; going through; classification; envelopment; sequence; trajectory; transformation; layering; infilling
Strategies - conversation; asking; planning; taking turns; estimating; co-operating; watching; role play; being with friends

---

Source: Arnold (1997: 241)

that represented what happened during a period of time and then using that as a structure to expand into a coherent story. In my case I used the points of reference or analytical frameworks as headings and produced one matrix for each child every three months. See Table 5.1 for an example.

Not only did I learn about how to reduce the data from Pollard's account, but in that first book there were five case study stories about individual children during their first three years at school, which were extremely illuminating both in terms of their experience and of how their stories were told. My favourite is 'Sally's Story' – Sally was the caretaker's daughter, so often spent extended hours at school and knew everyone. Here is a short excerpt:

Sally, Reception, relationships among friends and in the playground

Sally was one of the most popular children in the Reception class. She was very confident with other children and would often make the first move towards making friends with someone new. She particularly enjoyed 'looking after' new children and giving them guided tours of the school. Sometimes she might leave a slightly incorrect impression, explaining that, 'It's my Dad's school'. Mrs Gordon (Sally's mother) thought that she might suggest that 'Mrs Davison (head teacher) just thinks she runs the school. Daddy does it really'. Mr. Gordon (Sally's Dad) had had children come up and say 'Did you actually build the school?' (Mrs. Gordon, parent interview, March 1988, Reception).

(Pollard with Filer, 1996: 192)

Although this is, at one level, an amusing account about a child, it communicates a great deal about how Sally felt about school and how being the caretaker's daughter contributed to her overall sense of emotional well-being and confidence.

Reflecting on selecting material to include

- Put everything into chronological order – have I managed to do that? It also helps to use the child's exact age in all accounts.
- Become very familiar with all of the material – how familiar am I with all of the data?
- Practise highlighting or marking up what is significant and make notes of any new thoughts as they develop – have I managed to go through all of the data either highlighting, underlining or making notes of my developing thoughts?
- Reduce the data to one or more charts so the whole data set can be viewed at once – have I managed to put all of the essential information on to one or more charts to view?
- Use your chart(s) as a structure to expand your account into a coherent story that communicates well – how is the expansion into a story working?

The matrix can also be a way of showing how much data you have gathered. Table 5.2 gives an example from a later study, showing the data gathered about Susan (a pseudonym) and some main points about her learning.

Table 5.2 How observations can be viewed in an overview

Susan Date of Birth 13-11-00		
Date and Age	Length and Type of Obs	Summary of Action
31-10-03 2:11:18	2 hrs tracking/ narrative obs	Interest in going through marble run, funnel and garlic press. Putting money into till.
6-11-03 2:11:24	30 mins video obs	Using drill and saw to go through a boundary. Covering with cornflour and washing off. Near Annette. Denise off.
13-11-03 3:00:00	25 mins video obs	Playing in homecorner near other children. Staying near Angela. Denise there. Dad has been visiting.
28-11-03 3:00:15	35 mins video obs	Using computer and flipchart. Filling bottle with water through funnel. Near Annette. Denise off.
5-12-03 3:00:22	30 mins video obs	Using face paints, putting on and washing off. Transferring water from one container to another. Denise there.

(Continued)

Table 5.2 (Continued)

Susan Date of Birth 13-11-00

Date and Age	Length and Type of Obs	Summary of Action
8-12-03 3:00:25	31 mins video obs	Playing at sink, filling rubber glove with water. Washed Sihaya's hands and arms.
8-12-03 3:0:25	27 mins video obs	Grouptime with Denise. Susan enjoyed the action rhymes. Transferred water from one container to another.
19-04-04 3:05:06	16 mins video obs	At the sink, washing hands. Then manipulated 2 play people, drew horizontal lines, then sorted pencils by colour. Played in homecorner, pretending to wash up.
June 04	Home video	At Daniel's birthday and at the fair.
28-06-04	Meeting with Sian	Denise off longterm, replaced by Kirsty.
2-07-04 3:07:19	48 mins video obs	Ran marbles through a run, connected the run, trains and track. Interested in wheel/gates – rotational movement to facilitate going through. Face paint on hand and arm and story of Blue Balloon from Alison.
5-07-04	Meeting with Sian and Susan	
9-07-04 3:07:26	25 mins video obs	Grouptime with Kirsty. Visited the dining room in preparation for having lunch at nursery. Manipulated 2 play people and cloth. Reunion with her mother.
5-08-04 3:08:23	21 mins video obs	First day of having lunch at nursery. Helped self to food, worried about spilling water. Talked about Denise's baby. Outside on beach manipulating sand.
21-09-04 3:10:08	5 mins video obs	Susan learning to ride a two wheeler bicycle. Crashed and cried. Then continued practising.

Source: Arnold (2007: 426)

Issues to consider

- Am I familiar with the main literature in my area of study?
- Do I have certain points I want to make?
- Is my final study going to be a summary of my observations or am I going to use excerpts to put forward an argument or specific pieces of evidence?
- Is there any data that does not fit? If so, does it raise other questions that I can articulate?

6   Thinking about theory that illuminates learning

It is one thing to have educational principles. It is another to have theories. Having either or both is not enough. Teachers need to bring the two together and to create theory under-pinned by principles, and this requires highly educated professionals ... When theory and educational principles interact, practice makes progress.

(Bruce *et al.*, 1995: 52)

I would agree with Bruce that we need principles as well as theory in order to help us improve our practice. As far as I am concerned, my values and beliefs about children and how they learn are my prin-ciples. Applying this idea to Georgia, one of my firm principles was that she has valuable things to teach me. She did not arrive as a 'blank slate', but was seeking interaction from the beginning. I use theories to deepen my understanding of the knowledge she is seeking and of her ways of knowing. Schema theory helps me to understand the concepts she is exploring, and dispositional theory helps me to identify her ways of learning.

This chapter discusses:

- conceptual frameworks that might be used to make sense of the data and to illuminate learning
- schema theory
- the zone of proximal development
- dispositions to learn
- play
- curriculum frameworks.

Conceptual frameworks that might be used to make sense of the data

Introduction

Sometimes the terms 'theory' and 'framework' are used interchangeably. Usually a theory is used to refer to one idea or concept, and 'framework' to refer to a set of ideas. Using a 'framework' is generally more complex than using a 'theory' and integrates several ideas. However, as this is a 'grey area', in this book I would like to use 'conceptual framework' as an umbrella term to describe the theories and frameworks suggested that might assist in analysing and interpreting raw data gathered as part of a child observation study.

Conceptual frameworks you might use to illuminate children's learning

Within the field of early childhood, most research currently being produced builds on either the work of Piaget or the work of Vygotsky. These researchers are still the two 'giants' of early childhood research. Piaget believed that learning goes from 'inside to outside', with his strong emphasis on what children are biologically motivated to learn. Vygotsky saw the process going from 'outside to inside', with his strong emphasis on relationships and the co-construction of ideas between people. Both strongly supported the idea of 'constructivism' explored in Chapter 1 of this book, and Vygotsky's work expanded the idea or theory to become 'social constructivism'. I think that both ideas are valid, and subscribe to the idea that both processes are interacting, so children are motivated to explore what they are programmed to explore biologically and also influenced by the environment in which they grow up. They internalise ideas and learning from others – this is not pure imitation, but a process of construing or constructing whereby the child, as well as the adult or older child, offers ideas.

What have been most useful to me in studying young children are Piaget's theory of 'schemas' and Vygotsky's theory of the 'zone of proximal development', so they are the first two conceptual frameworks considered here.

Schema theory as a conceptual framework

Piaget's big idea was that our actions become our thoughts. Athey (2007: 46) comments that, 'The associated notion [at the heart of Piaget's theories] that 'thought' is 'internalised action' has been slow to be adopted as a research hypothesis, probably because it is difficult to test.'

Following Piaget's ideas translated into English is still fairly difficult, but Athey made his work accessible and made a heroic attempt to help the reader to see how our actions become our thoughts in Chapter 6 of her seminal text *Extending Thought in Young Children* (Athey, 2007). Athey offers several definitions of 'schema'. I favour this one drawn from Piaget and Inhelder (1973: 382): 'The function of a schema is to enable generalisations to be made about objects and events in the environment to which a schema is applied.' In my own words, schemas are repeated patterns of action. Sometimes those actions have effects that can be seen – for example, lines or circles drawn in the sand as a result of a particular action with a finger or stick or foot. This is the figurative effect of the action. Matthews (2003: 23) describes schemas as follows: 'When the same, or similar action is applied in different contexts and upon different objects, the child receives valuable information about the object and how the movement has affected the object.'

Matthews, drawing on brain research, reports that 'neuroscience suggests that the human perceptual system is divided into two kinds, one devoted to finding out where things are, while another finds out what things are' – in essence, the '*movement* and *shape* of objects is being perceived' as we explore (2003: 25). This idea makes sense to me. A classic experiment carried out by young children is dropping objects from a high chair or pram to the floor. If adults cooperate, then they will keep returning the objects to the child, so that the child can repeat their actions. If a variety of objects are provided to drop, then different effects will be observed. If you pay close attention to the child's actions, they often track the downward movement and then stare down at the shape created by the object when it lands, demonstrating their interest in movement and shape. The movement is usually described as a 'dynamic vertical' trajectory. Different writers may describe the patterns observed slightly differently but that is less important than seeing the same pattern repeated with different materials and in different contexts.

Examples of common schemas observed

- **Trajectory:** moving in straight lines, arcs or curves.
- **Lines:** representing lines by lining up objects or by making marks.
- **Transporting:** carrying objects or being carried from one place to another. Frequently involves gathering and distributing.
- **Heaping:** gathering materials into a heap.
- **Scattering:** the seemingly random distribution of materials by scattering (the opposite of heaping).
- **Enclosing:** enclosing oneself, an object or space.
- **Enveloping:** enveloping or covering oneself, an object or space.

- **Containing:** putting materials or oneself inside an object capable of containing.
- **Going through a boundary:** causing oneself or some material to go through a boundary and emerge on the other side.
- **Positioning:** children position themselves differently – for example, 'on top' or 'upside down' – in order to view the world from a different position; they also place objects in different positions.
- **Rotating:** turning, twisting or rolling oneself or objects in the environment around. See Figure 6.1 for examples of objects that rotate.
- **Connecting:** children become interested in connecting themselves to objects or other people and objects to one another; they may connect hair to heads in their drawings.
- **Making a one-to-one correspondence:** placing objects, for example, one in each space, or acting on objects or people in a one-to-one correspondence (as in counting).

Source: Arnold (1997)

Figure 6.1 Examples of two objects that children might notice rotating

Drawing on the idea of constructivism, the processes of learning that we can identify in coming to know about things are 'assimilation', 'accommodation' and 'equilibrium'. As human beings, we are always searching for patterns and connections. When we are trying out a pattern of action (or, in other words, a schema), we try it out on objects in our environment that look likely to behave in the way we expect (Arnold, 2014). Some of the time, our expectation of what will happen is confirmed and we 'assimilate' new content into our current structure or view of the world. So, going back to the baby in the high chair or pram, they may drop a variety of objects that always fall in a downward trajectory and land on the floor near them. They may 'assimilate' cutlery, keys, napkins, etc., into that pattern with only slight variations. Then they may be given or may select a bouncy ball, which bounces back up towards them when dropped. This result may perturb them and may result in the 'accommodation' of some new learning. They will probably want to drop the ball several times to check that the result is always the same, and gradually they will 'accommodate' to the idea that some objects rebound when dropped. At this point, they will be more settled, or in 'equilibrium', and no longer perturbed by what happens. The advantage of knowing about which schemas a young child is currently exploring is in the opportunity to offer more and wider content to feed their interest in particular actions.

Children also coordinate schemas and are interested in coordinations. Figure 6.2 shows Nicole and Gabriella enjoying going 'up and down' and 'round and round' simultaneously.

Figure 6.2 Nicole and Gabriella going 'up and down' and 'round and round'

Although actions are very important, schemas are also explored through symbols, through functional dependency relationships and through thinking. '**Symbolic representations** use actions, mark making and other graphic forms and speech' (Athey, 2012: 9).

For example, actions become **symbolic** when young children use one thing to stand for another – a commonly observed example is using any object as a phone. When Georgia called a 20p coin a 'Choo choo' this was directly related to her experience of the ride (action). It was, for her, a symbol of the ride. So the 20p was in place of the ride and the name she gave it also signified the ride. When young children make marks, at first the mark is related to the action – for example, 'up/down' or possibly 'round and round'. After a while and when they notice the effects of their actions, they may name the mark. At this point, it becomes a symbol. For example Harry made marks depicting his dad's journey to work (Figure 6.3). His drawing is still closely related to the action but is symbolic of his dad's journey because he explains and names it as his father's journey to work.

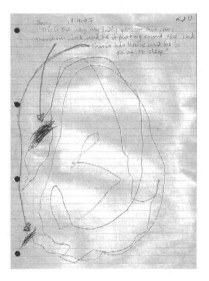

Figure 6.3 At 4y 4m, Harry's map
Source: Arnold (2003: 119)

Athey defines that '**functional dependency relationships** are based on actions with their effects', so functional dependency relationships are about the effect of a person's actions on objects or people (2012: 9).

For example, when

> Harry (aged 3y) discovers that it is easier to gets objects to go over the fence from an elevated position (that is, standing on a chair and throwing), he is using the up/down schema at a *functional dependency level*. The object going over the fence is functionally dependent on the power and angle of the throw.
>
> (Arnold, 2003: 43)

Thinking is a bit trickier to detect. In the Froebel Project, Athey and her team adopted a 'definition of thought' as 'when children were able to recall and represent events about people and objects without needing concrete reminders of the original experience' (Athey, 2012: 9). Moments when we see children thinking are often signalled by their body language and subsequent actions, so I would like to have a broader view, obviously supported by the evidence of close observation. My recent observations of Gabriella, when she was under 2y (Arnold, 2014), include several where we are in a situation we have been in before: she holds her index finger up and looks intent, and then dashes off to get something she has remembered. As far as I am concerned, this is evidence of her thinking about a previous experience and wanting to repeat it. There is, of course, a reminder in the form of the location.

Using schema theory to apply to my observations

- Are children's schemas of interest to me?
- How might I apply some of the theory presented above to my observations?
- Will I be able to show a child assimilating fresh content into an existing pattern?
- In what ways can I support a child's learning with knowing about schemas?

Further reading

Arnold, C. (2003) *Observing Harry: Child Development and Learning 0–5 years*. Maidenhead: Open University Press.

Atherton, F. and Nutbrown, C. (2013) *Understanding Schemas and Young Children*. London: Sage.

Athey, C. (2007) *Extending Thought in Young Children: A Parent–Teacher Partnership*, 2nd edn. London: Paul Chapman.

Mairs, K. and the Pen Green Team (2012) *Young Children Learning Through Schemas* (ed. Arnold, C.). Oxford: Routledge.

The 'zone of proximal development' as a conceptual framework

Vygotsky's big idea was that children learn from being part of a social context. He saw the whole environment as leading development. He explains how meaning is constructed between people before being 'internalised':

A good example of this process may be found in the development of pointing. Initially, this gesture is nothing more than an unsuccessful attempt to grasp something, a movement aimed at a certain object which designates forthcoming activity. The child attempts to grasp an object beyond his reach; his hands, stretched toward that object, remain poised in the air ... When the mother comes to the child's aid and realizes his movement means something, the situation changes fundamentally. Pointing becomes a gesture for others.

(Vygotsky, 1978: 56)

This simple example shows how, particularly with young children, adults respond to what we think are the child's intentions. Gradually children internalise an idea and it becomes part of their repertoire through which they communicate with others: 'An interpersonal process is transformed into an intrapersonal one' (Vygotsky, 1978: 57).

Vygotsky claimed that a similar process can be observed with speech – that is, what is heard externally becomes internalised, making the social context very important for learning. He and colleagues 'developed the hypothesis that children's egocentric (self-centred and spoken aloud to oneself) speech should be regarded as the transitional form between external and internal speech' (Vygotsky, 1978: 26). He further explains that, 'Functionally, egocentric speech is the basis for inner speech, while in its external form it is embedded in communicative speech' (1978: 26). So, according to Vygotsky, thinking and planning begin externally before being internalised, or, to put it into a nutshell, **our interactions become our thinking**.

Vygotsky disagreed with the idea that development leads learning. He was convinced that learning can lead development. Vygotsky states that, 'A well known and empirically established fact is that learning should be matched in some manner with the child's developmental level' (1978: 85). However, he argued that what is generally tested is the 'actual developmental level', when what would be more appropriate to test would be the 'future developmental level' or 'what a child can do with assistance today', so the 'buds of development' rather than the 'fruits of development' (Vygotsky, 1978: 86).

Vygotsky died aged 38 in 1934, but many researchers have continued to develop his ideas, particularly in relation to the 'zone of proximal development', which is how he described the burgeoning abilities of children. Vygotsky used experimental methods that were in vogue at that time and so have some of his followers. Bruner has taken forward some of Vygotsky's research and has suggested that adults, or older or more capable peers, can 'scaffold' children's learning. While this is a good idea, I am not sure whether it is well understood. I discuss 'scaffolding' in a recently published paper:

'Scaffolding' is used as a metaphor to describe the role of a more capable person, when interacting with a child, who has the potential to find a solution or to solve a problem. I believe this concept has not been well understood and often the adult agenda takes over, rather than the adult trying to understand the child's intentions.

(Arnold, 2014: 2)

For me, the 'zone of proximal development' leads me to think about what a child may be interested in and motivated to learn next. The 'scaffold' needs to be fairly flexible as I work out how I can offer just the right amount of help or support. Considering a child's zone of proximal development (zpd) also involves considering the pedagogical approaches of those supporting the child. Although, occasionally, it may be appropriate to 'tell' or 'demonstrate' how to do something, there always seems to be a lot more value and lasting learning when children discover how to do something for themselves. According to Athey (2007: 44), 'The teacher, therefore, must arrange things so that knowledge is actively constructed and not simply copied.' Athey goes on to explain that what we need to focus on understanding are the concepts that children are working on. For example, when Georgia queried something she heard me saying by asking 'Pay golf?' I knew that she was working on the concept of paying for things. She may also only have had a very vague idea of what 'golf' is. It would be no good explaining to her at 2y 5m. She could, however, learn from the experience of going to the golf club and seeing people pay their money before teeing off. She still would not fully understand but the experience would contribute something to her current understanding. If Georgia was in a setting, we could set up a role-play experience, so that she and other children could share and extend their knowledge.

Using the 'zone of proximal development' to apply to my observations

- Does identifying a child's zpd appeal to me?
- How can I observe what children can do with assistance?
- Do I need to focus on the meaning being made between children and between children and adults?
- How can I tell whether the adult or more capable peer is in tune with the child's interest?
- Does identifying the zpd always involve observing a child in interaction with others?

Further reading

Daniels, H. (2001) *Vygotsky and Pedagogy*. Oxford: Routledge.

Vygotsky, L.S. (1978) *Mind in Society: The Development of Higher Psychological Processes*. London: Harvard University Press.

'Dispositions to learn' as a conceptual framework

I first heard about 'dispositions' or 'habits of mind' in a talk by Lilian Katz more than 20 years ago. It made sense to me that we should be giving attention to not only *what* children are learning about, but *how* children are learning. Around that time, ideas about learning styles and emotional intelligence also came to the fore. These, too, are concepts concerned with how we approach learning rather than what subject knowledge we gain. It could be said that the time had come to articulate what may have been in the minds of many educators for some time.

I believe 'dispositions' as a conceptual framework has endured partly because of the research in New Zealand on fostering positive dispositions to learn, and recording them in Learning Stories – an idea many early childhood settings in the UK have imported (Carr and Lee, 2012) – and partly because we are living in a rapidly changing technological age. We literally have information or knowledge at our fingertips and therefore how to access information, which is constantly being updated, seems more important than the information itself.

The New Zealand early childhood curriculum, Te Whāriki, is not based on subject areas, but on the following four principles.

1   **Empowerment:** the early childhood curriculum empowers the child to learn and grow.
2   **Holistic development:** the early childhood curriculum reflects the holistic way children learn and grow.
3   **Family and community:** the wider world of family and community is an integral part of the early childhood curriculum.
4   **Relationships:** children learn through responsive and reciprocal relationships with people, places, and things.

(Ministry of Education, 1996: 14)

The following strands 'arise from the four [above] principles: Well-being; Belonging; Contribution; Communication; Exploration' (1996: 16). Goals arise from the principles and strands. This curriculum has a very different feel to one based on traditional subject areas, although there is some overlap with personal, social and emotional development, and in the Early Years Foundation Stage (EYFS) 'Characteristics of Effective Learning'.

The Ministry's website explains that:

Teachers are foregrounding dispositional learning by describing learning as being able to try something new, being playful, persisting, using trial and error, making mistakes, choosing hard work, keeping going when things get tough, being brave and curious.

(Ministry of Education, n.d.: 1)

A simple definition of 'disposition' is offered by Da Ros-Voseles and Fowler-Haughey, researchers working in America, in a paper entitled 'Why children's dispositions should matter to all teachers' (2007): 'Dispositions are frequent and voluntary habits of thinking and doing' (2007: 1). They also point out that, 'when people describe good teachers, they mention dispositions such as being accepting, stimulating, and encouraging' (2007: 4). So dispositions are human behaviour, and can be positive or negative and applied to anyone of any age.

Carr *et al.* (2009) report on a wide range of studies, some of which use slightly different terms, but the broad meaning is similar, from 'mindsets' (Dweck, 2006) to 'learning power' (Claxton, 2002). They describe this wide range of dispositions in the literature as 'dispositions that focus more on the "mind" than the 'environment' (2009: 15). Carr *et al.* challenge the view that dispositions are 'within-child' qualities or features. They say that 'learning includes knowing why, knowing when and where and knowing how to use knowledge and ability' (2009: 16). Carr *et al.* further explain that, 'An aspect of all learning is, in a sense, learning to "read" situations: recognising when to speak, when to be silent, when to ask questions.' So, in their view, children have to know when it is appropriate to use certain dispositions, and the environment in which children find themselves needs to 'afford' those dispositions for them to be used successfully.

Although there is no definitive list of dispositions, in their 2009 book, Carr *et al.* settle on three broad areas to be encouraged: 'reciprocity, resilience and imagination', and further link those nouns to the following verbs:

- establishing a dialogue
- being and becoming a group member
- initiating and orchestrating projects
- asking questions
- exploring possible worlds
- storying selves.

(Carr *et al.*, 2009: 32)

Like any conceptual framework, the use of dispositions needs to be underpinned by a philosophy and an understanding of children learning. There are some really illuminating case studies in Carr *et al.*'s book, which are carried out longitudinally over 18 months and give rounded pictures of each child's approach to learning. Karen Daniels, carrying out an action research study in the UK, expresses concern that, 'because the effectiveness of the learning stories centres around capturing positive snapshots of a child's learning experience', this may 'create an illusion that all children have high levels of social competence and a range of positive learning dispositions that are continually displayed' (2013: 305). This issue is certainly one that has bothered me previously when I have read Learning Stories that contain a lot of enthusiastic comments from workers. That method could be seen as 'sanitising' accounts of children's learning. Another concern I picked up from Daniels' paper was that picking out positive dispositions could also be used as a sort of behaviour management technique.

One strong critic of the approach has written several papers questioning whether Learning Stories are a robust enough method of assessing children's learning. He suggests 'learning notes' carried out more frequently and written very close to the event, 'without bias', would be a more effective way of documenting children's learning (Blaiklock, 2010: 6).

Without a definitive list, it might be interesting and helpful to define what a child is repeatedly doing that helps them learn, from the observations you have carried out. I would argue that different qualities and related actions are valued by different people. For example, 'maintaining attention, concentrating and sitting quietly' is a goal for 40–60+ months in the DfE document 'Early Years Outcomes' currently used as a guide in England (2013). This behaviour may be highly prized in some settings and less so in others.

Using 'dispositions to learn' to apply to my observations

- Do I have a sound understanding of what is meant by 'dispositions to learn'?
- Are they something we have discussed in our setting?
- Do we have an agreed list of dispositions we want to encourage?
- What would these dispositions look like?
- Or is this child observation study designed to explore the dispositions children are using in our setting?

Further reading

Carr, M., Smith, A.B., Duncan, J., Jones, C., Lee, W. and Marshall, K. (2009) *Learning in the Making: Disposition and Design in Early Education.* Rotterdam: Sense Publishers.

Claxton, G. and Carr, M. (2004) A framework for teaching learning: the dynamics of disposition. *Early Years*, 24(1), March, 87–97.

Dweck, C.S. (2000) *Self-Theories: Their Role in Motivation, Personality, and Development.* East Sussex: Taylor & Francis.

Dweck, C.S. and Leggett, E.L. (1988) A social-cognitive approach to motivation and personality. *Psychological Review*, 95, 256–273.

Play

Play is a broad and complex subject and one not easily defined. A good starting point might be you and your team's experience of play as children and what your accounts have in common. Sutton-Smith (2009: 1) states that, 'We all play occasionally, and we all know what playing feels like. But when it comes to making theoretical statements about what play is, we fall into silliness. There is little agreement among us and much ambiguity.'

Actually, this view fits rather well with constructivism as a theory of knowing rather than a theory of knowledge, as each person's individual experience of play must be different even if there are features that seem similar. It is those invariant features that many researchers and theorists have tried to capture.

The two 'giants' referred to earlier in this chapter, Piaget and Vygotsky, both had views and wrote about their ideas of what play is. Piaget (1951: 147) accepted that 'the phenomenon is difficult to understand'. Drawing on his observations of his own children, he came to the conclusion that, 'if adapted activity and thought constitute an equilibrium between assimilation and accommodation, play begins as soon as there is predominance of assimilation' (1951: 150).

At that time, Piaget saw play as consolidating what is being assimilated through practice. He saw play as 'practice for its own sake, the "pleasure of being the cause" so well described by K. Groos' (1951: 153). He firmly believed that play is 'exercise' and not 'pre-exercise'. Athey supported this view in saying that you 'play' with something only when you know it well.

Vygotsky, on the other hand, stated that, 'play creates a zone of proximal development of the child. In play a child always behaves beyond his average age, above his daily behavior; in play it is as though he were a head taller than himself' (1978: 102).

Vygotsky thought that in play children behave in advance of their development and pointed out that, 'A child's greatest self-control occurs in play' because of the demands of the play rules (1978: 99). Vygotsky said that all play contains rules and that, even in an 'imaginary situation', players create rules about how to carry out roles. This may be the child's or children's current concept of the rules of that situation but, nevertheless, according to Vygotsky, the rules exist.

Both Piaget and Vygotsky acknowledged that children need to play and that play serves a therapeutic function in helping children understand their experiences.

Winnicott's discussion of play is much more rooted in the psychoanalytic ideas of play and play as a therapy for disturbed infants and adults. Winnicott's explanation builds on his work on transitional objects and phenomena. He saw play as beginning in the space between mother and baby:

> The playground is a potential space between the mother and the baby or joining mother and baby.

> Play is immensely exciting. It is exciting *not primarily because the instincts are involved*, be it understood! The thing about playing is always the precariousness of the interplay of personal psychic reality and the experience of control of actual objects.
>
> (Winnicott, 1971, in Caldwell and Joyce, 2011: 242)

Although Winnicott was a psychoanalyst, he saw the value of play for everyone and did not necessarily 'use' play in his practice. He observed that when children (and adults) are able to play, then most problems are resolved through play. He saw 'playing' as 'the continuous evidence of creativity, which means aliveness' (Caldwell and Joyce, 2011: 231). Caldwell and Joyce (2011: 232) observe that, 'Playing in Winnicott's usage involves a relation with, and a care of, the self. It is a form of living well.'

These contrasting views make it doubly difficult to study 'play' and to use 'play' as a concept to understand children's actions. Tina Bruce (1991, 2001, 2004) offers a comprehensive review: the '12 features of free-flow play', which 'emerged from the wealth of literature that exists on play either in English or translated into English' (2004: 148).

'The 12 features of free-flow play' (adapted from Bruce, 1991; Bruce, 2004: 149)

1   In their play children use the first-hand experiences they have had in life.

2   Play does not conform to pressures to conform to external rules, outcomes, purposes or directions. Because of this, children keep control of their lives in their play.

3   Play is a process. It has no products. When the play ends, it vanishes as quickly as it arrived.

4   Children choose to play. It is intrinsically motivated. It arises when the conditions are conducive, spontaneously, and it is sustained as it flows.

5   Children rehearse the future in their play. Play helps children to learn to function, in advance of what they can do in the present.

6   Play takes children into a world of pretend. They imagine other worlds, creating stories of possible and impossible worlds beyond the here and now in the past, present and future, and it transforms them into different characters.

7   Play can be solitary, and this sort of play is often very deep. Children learn who they are, and how to face and deal with their ideas, feelings, relationships and physical bodies.

8   Children and/or adults can play together, in parallel (companionship play), associatively or cooperatively in pairs or groups.

9   Play can be initiated by a child or an adult, but adults need to bear in mind that every player has his or her own personal play agenda (which he/she may be unaware of), and to respect this by not insisting that the adult agenda should dominate the play.

10   Children's free-flow play is characterised by deep concentration, and it is difficult to distract them from their learning. Children at play wallow in their learning.

> 11 In play children try out their recent learning, mastery, competencies and skills, and consolidate them. They use their technical prowess and confidently apply their learning.
>
> 12 Children at play coordinate their ideas and feelings, and make sense of relationships with family, friends and culture. Play is an integrating mechanism, which allows flexible, adaptive, imaginative, innovative behaviour. Play makes children into whole people, able to keep balancing their lives in a fast-changing world.

According to Bruce, if several of the features are present in children's play, then free-flow play is occurring, so this could be used as a framework to discuss a child's play as part of a child observation study.

Using 'play' as a framework to apply to my observations

- How would you judge that a child is playing?
- How close is their play to a real experience?
- In your observations, would you say that children are learning through their interactions, which results in behaviour ahead of their development?
- Do the children you are observing seem to be practising recently acquired skills or knowledge?

Further reading

Bruce, T. (2004) *Developing Learning in Early Childhood*. London: Paul Chapman.

Caldwell, L. and Joyce, A. (eds) (2011) *Reading Winnicott*. London: Routledge.

Piaget, J. (1951) *Play, Dreams and Imitation in Childhood*. London: William Heinemann Ltd.

Vygotsky, L.S. (1978) *Mind in Society: The Development of Higher Psychological Processes*. London: Harvard University Press.

Curriculum frameworks

If you make detailed observations of children when they are deeply engaged, any curriculum framework can be applied to your observations.

Aistear (the early childhood curriculum in Ireland)

Aistear is the early childhood curriculum in Ireland for children from birth to 6 years. Like the New Zealand Curriculum (Te Whāriki), Aistear is bilingual and focuses on 'a set of principles of early learning and development', and the four themes of 'Well-being; Identity and Belonging; Communicating; and, Exploring and Thinking' (NCCA, 2009: 5). Each theme has four aims, and each aim has a set of expressed learning goals and examples of how adults might support learning across the age range. Here is an example of one of the four aims and the related learning goals within the theme of well-being:

Aim 1.

Children will be strong psychologically and socially.

Learning Goals

In partnership with the adult, children will

1 Make strong attachments and develop warm and supportive relationships with family, peers and adults in out-of-home settings and in their community
2 Be aware of and name their own feelings, and understand that others may have different feelings
3 Handle transitions and changes well
4 Be confident and self-reliant
5 Respect themselves, others and the environment
6 Make decisions and choices about their own learning and development.

(NCCA, 2009: 17)

These are very ambitious aims that, I think, would need a high level of training to implement. Nevertheless, examples and advice about practice follow, and could be used to begin to think about practice that supports young children.

The Early Years Foundation Stage Curriculum (EYFS) (the UK early years curriculum)

The most recent version of this curriculum framework (DfE, 2014) states that:

Every child deserves the best possible start in life and the support that enables them to fulfil their potential. Children develop quickly in the early years and a child's experiences between birth and age five have a major impact on their future life chances. A secure, safe and happy childhood is important in its own right. Good parenting and high quality early learning together provide the foundation children need to make the most of their abilities and talents as they grow up.

(2014: 5)

Again, these are ambitious goals for young children. The curriculum requirements have recently changed from six areas, which were considered
equally, to three prime areas and four specific areas. These are all 'areas
of learning' or, in other words, subject areas. The three prime areas are
'Communication and language; Physical development; and, Personal, social
and emotional development'. These three areas are currently considered
most important for development. These are the three areas reported on to
parents at the 'Progress Check between two and three' (DfE, 2014: 13).
Practitioners can report on other areas that are areas of strength or areas
for development, but that is at their discretion. Just to give a sense of what
are the goals:

> **Personal, social and emotional development** involves helping
> children to develop a positive sense of themselves, and others; to
> form positive relationships and develop respect for others; to develop
> social skills and learn how to manage their feelings; to understand
> appropriate behaviour in groups; and to have confidence in their
> own abilities.
>
> (2014: 8)

The 'specific areas' of the EYFS are: 'Literacy; Mathematics; Understanding the world; Expressive arts and design'. The curriculum document can be
downloaded from the following website: www.foundationyears.org.uk.

Curricula do change and develop quite frequently according to gov-
ernment legislation, and the current values and beliefs being promoted, but
the important point to be held in mind when carrying out a child observation
study is that detailed observations of children, who are deeply involved, tell
us a great deal about their learning, and any goals can be compared with
what we see children doing that helps us to assess their learning in specific
areas.

Using curricula as frameworks to apply to my observations

- Is it important to know how children are experiencing the
  curriculum in my setting?
- Do the observations provide evidence that the child or
  children are reaching the learning goals articulated in the
  document?
- Can we add more information to how children reach these
  learning goals?
- Are there goals that are inappropriate?

Further reading

Department for Education (2013) *Early Years Outcomes*. Crown Copyright.
Department for Education (2014) *Statutory Framework for the Early Years Foundation Stage*. Crown Copyright.
Ministry of Education (1996) *Te Whariki: Early Childhood Curriculum*. Wellington, New Zealand: Learning Media Ltd.
NCCA (2009) *Aistear: The Early Childhood Curriculum Framework*. Dublin: NCCA.

In the next chapter the frameworks explored here are applied to observations of Philip.

Issues to consider

- Which frameworks appeal to me?
- What do I want to learn more about?
- How can I understand more about this child's learning?
- What will illuminate this child's learning?
- How will a theoretical framework inform my pedagogy?

7 Analysing and interpreting what the information gathered is telling us

> Analysis involves 'a detailed examination of the parts' of a piece of data and interpretation involves an 'explanation' of what the data might mean.
>
> (Tulloch, 1993)
>
> Chris Athey told me a wonderful story about speaking at a conference about her research findings, a member of the audience asking 'So what?', and then having to spend several more years working on the interpretation and implications for practice before publication (Athey, personal communication, 2005).
>
> Analysis and interpretation is a really important part of the process when you examine your data. Using the conceptual frameworks described in Chapter 6 can help you understand more about what seems to be happening and about the learning for the child.

This chapter introduces a sequence of observations of Philip (aged 20–22 months), then a video observation of Georgia (aged 3y 9m 2d):

- First, we consider three observations of Philip aged 20–22 months, taken from Harriet Johnson's *Children in the Nursery School* (1928/72) and apply the conceptual frameworks described in Chapter 6 to the sequence of observations in turn. These are: schema theory; the zone of proximal development; dispositions to learn; play; curriculum frameworks.
- Second, we consider a video observation of Georgia, and apply the frameworks of 'involvement', 'well-being' and 'schemas' to the observation.

Philip and the slide

Some context: 'Philip was twenty months old when he entered the nursery school … he was undisturbed when his mother left … He runs with a babylike waddle, tipping from side to side, feet wide apart, so that he has a broad stance … He goes about with a smile as if in anticipation of the next delightful experience' (Johnson, 1928/72: 170). (The indoor slide referred to below is higher and steeper than the outdoor slide referred to.)

The observations

20 months – Philip walked for several steps up the chute out of doors, holding the slide – slipped and repeated. Walked up four steps of the indoor slide in company with others of the group.

21 months – Walked up the steps of the out-of-door slide – smiling. He stepped up a bit over the top, but with a little help he got his second leg over without its getting caught. He seated himself beaming and held the side of the chute. He was held back by adult so that the speed would not alarm him, and slid, squealing with joy. He sat at the foot, then scrabbled up the chute, climbed on as far as he could reach from the side. He *did not go back* to the steps and paid no attention to the 3-steps which were placed at the side so that he could get on the chute from them.

22 months – Philip went down the out-of-door slide on his stomach, feet first, after turning himself over on top from the normal sitting position. Indoors he has been given the usual pattern of lying down at the top of the chute, turning over and making the descent feet first on his stomach. One day he evaded control and went down sitting. He could not at first nor always maintain an upright position so he went hurtling down with one leg in the air and almost over the edge. It filled him with intense elation and he showed no signs of reluctance or trepidation … He rose, laughing loudly and squealing, ran to the steps again. He repeated several times and was able to keep the upright position for part of the time. He sat poised at the top and thumped the chute with his heels once or twice. He has also been practising going down the slide steps both facing out and backing down. (Johnson, 1928/72: 171–173)

Using schema theory as a framework to understand

(Schemas are italicised.)

Philip's interest seemed to be in the *dynamic vertical trajectory* or, to be more precise, the *oblique trajectory* provided by two quite challenging pieces of equipment. He was exploring *up and down* through his actions. At 20 months he ventured no further than going *up* several of the steps of each slide.

At 21 months Philip climbed right to the *top* of the outdoor slide and experienced being *on top* and seeing the environment from that different perspective. He slid *down* and immediately attempted to climb *up* the chute, rather than repeating the whole sequence of actions, that is, going *up* the steps and being *on top* and then sliding *down*. Johnson interpreted his immediate action of trying to climb *up* the chute as 'an example of immaturity in the perceptual pattern' (1928/72: 171). It was as though he was not holding in mind the sequence of actions and the fact that *going up the steps* led to an opportunity to *go down the slide*. I have observed this happen previously on a piece of Pen Green video when a child was building high with hollow blocks and a worker offered him some steps so he could reach to build higher. After accepting the offer of the step ladder, he, at first, walked past it and repeated his action of trying to reach *up* to add another block to his tower. It was only when the worker explained and gestured to him that he could climb *up* the ladder in order to place the next block on his tower that he accommodated that information. The function of the ladder was to enable him to climb higher. Similarly, Philip may not have at first held in mind the function of the steps, which was to enable him to reach the top of the slide.

At 22 months Philip varied his way of *sliding down* the outdoor slide by sliding down on his stomach and feet first, which feels entirely different to sitting up. The *oblique* angle is experienced with the whole body when lying down and there is no adjustment or conscious adaptation of the body to the slope in the way that there is when sitting up.

At the same age, Philip experimented with going *down* the steeper indoor slide sitting up, having been encouraged to go *down* lying down. That first journey sounded quite precarious as it was so steep that he could not 'always maintain an upright position' (1928/72: 173). By this time, Philip had accommodated the whole sequence of actions, so immediately 'ran to the steps again' and repeated his actions 'several times' (1928/72: 173).

I wondered whether 'thumping the chute with his heels' was a way of establishing his sitting up position. In earlier observations, Johnson had noted that Philip had some knowledge of how to use his body to increase his stability both when walking 'with a broad stance' and on the slide when he used his feet on the sides to keep control of his speed (1928/72: 170).

Finally, we are told that Philip was also practising going *down* the steps facing out and backing down. So Philip was gradually finding as many different ways as possible of moving *up and down* both slides. It is this wealth of experiences that feeds schemas and thinking.

Atherton and Nutbrown (2013: 68) present observations of a child exploring a dynamic vertical schema. He seemed intent on pushing a pram and then a bike up a slide. Within a schematic frame, it was recognised that he was experiencing and extending his knowledge of force (the pram is light so requires minimal effort to push), ascending and descending trajectories (moving up and down the slide with the pram), height (the pram is above his head and his arms are raised), position (up to the top and down to the bottom), weight (the pram is light and can be pushed to the top of the slide easily) …

(2013: 69)

Athey (2007: 51) points out that, 'what is "known" leads to what becomes "better known"'.

Using the 'zone of proximal development' as a framework to understand

At 20 months we notice that Philip 'walked up the slide in company with others from the group'. This suggests that he was influenced by what he saw other children do, and that he wanted to join in. One debate about his actions is whether or not this constitutes pure imitation. I am inclined to think that children's actions and thinking are a little more complex than pure imitation. Furthermore, most children do not just blindly follow or copy what other people in their environment are doing. For a start, they need to notice what others are doing. Then, they need to be attracted to what others are doing. Third, what other people are doing needs to be within their capabilities, which is where I think the zone of proximal development comes in. So Philip was indeed noticing. He was obviously attracted by the actions of the group and he judged that he, too, could climb up the steps. We do not know of his other experiences of steps or stairs, but the likelihood is that he had some experience of stairs at home.

At 21 months Philip managed to go further, so in Vygotsky's terms, at 20 months, Philip's zone of actual development in relation to this equipment was going up several steps (on the outdoor slide) and four steps (on the indoor slide). However, he probably could have achieved more with the help of an adult, resulting in the identification of his zone of proximal development. At 21 months, Philip could climb to the top, but did not have a great deal of awareness of the angle of the slope and the effect of sliding down, so the adult 'held him back' so that the experience would not be off-putting. This was interesting as I usually think of the adult role as supporting children to move forward when, in this case, it involved 'holding him back', literally and physically. This shows how complex the adult role is in relation to supporting young children's learning. Another adult might have stopped Philip from having a go on the slide, but I get the feeling, in this setting, that the children were fairly autonomous decision makers. So the beliefs and values of the adults are apparent in their actions, and need to be shared and explicit, as well as implicitly embedded in their actions and interactions (see the Introduction).

When Philip 'climbed as far as he could reach' at 21 months, he was demonstrating his zone of actual development, or what he could achieve without help. Each worker or parent might regard this situation differently. Is it a good idea to assist a child to go beyond what they can do today, especially with regard to climbing up a slide?

At 22 months, Philip 'evaded control' and went down the very steep indoor slide sitting up. This seemed to be beyond his zone of actual development but within his zone of proximal development. So he took control and went 'hurtling down with one leg in the air and almost over the edge'. Philip really enjoyed taking that risk and seemed to work within his zpd while practising before he was able to 'keep upright for part of the time', at which point his actions on the indoor slide became his actual developmental level.

Then he began to experiment with and to practise going down the steps 'facing out' and 'backing down'. This was the next challenge he set himself and an example of what was in his zpd. It is interesting to think about the adult 'scaffolding' a child's learning in the context of these observations of Philip. It may be that the group scaffolded his learning by using the slides each day in his presence. That would fit with Vygotsky's idea that we internalise experiences from our cultural context. The adult did play a role in making sure that Philip had a good experience and did not hurt himself, but that is a much more subtle role than many adults take on with young children.

Using 'dispositions to learn' as a framework to understand

(Dispositions are underlined.)

First, I went through the observations to get a sense of how Philip was conducting himself when engaging. So I used a sort of 'open coding', marking anything that I thought indicated how Philip approached learning.

Even the description of the context indicated that Philip was trusting and eager to learn. I thought he might be sociable as he 'walked up four steps of the indoor slide in company with others of the group'. He initiated his own learning and took great pleasure in tackling new skills. In this sequence of observations, he was a risk-taker although, being quite young, he was not always aware of the consequences of his actions. Philip showed that he was confident, curious and could persevere.

This open coding gave me a list of ideas that I could use subsequently to expand or reduce when considering further observations of Philip. Through looking at more observations of Philip, I could establish which were his 'frequent and voluntary habits of thinking and doing' (Da Ros-Voseles and Fowler-Haughey, 2007: 1).

Then I looked at the work of Carr *et al.* (2009) and thought about whether Philip was displaying any of the dispositions they name. The three broad areas of 'reciprocity, resilience and imagination' can be linked with Philip's approach.

At only 20 months, he was already joining in with the group on one occasion in this sequence of observations. This and his general sunny outlook boded well for developing a <u>reciprocal</u> approach to learning. Although not explicitly stated, Philip must have been interacting with the adults when he was, for example, 'beaming'. Also, when he 'sat poised at the top' of the slide, the observer was noticing Philip's actions, and the chances are that Philip was noticing the observer and interacting, if only in a small way.

There was evidence of Philip showing '<u>resilience</u>', particularly when he took a risk and 'hurtled down' the slide. His response to that experience was 'intense elation' and 'no sign of reluctance or trepidation'. He could take the risk of being 'almost over the edge' in his stride, which amounts to demonstrating <u>resilience</u>.

Philip showed '<u>imagination</u>' in coming up with ideas of how to vary his explorations on both slides. He did not necessarily take up the adult's ideas, for example when '3-steps were placed at the side', but that may have been because he did not understand the significance of the 3-steps, which would have enabled him to get onto the slide halfway down.

I also considered the verbs used by Carr *et al.* in describing the dispositions:

- establishing a dialogue
- being and becoming a group member
- initiating and orchestrating projects
- asking questions
- exploring possible worlds
- storying selves.

(Carr *et al.*, 2009: 32)

Establishing a dialogue

If we think of establishing a dialogue in a broad sense, Philip was interacting with the adults and with the group through his actions.

Being and becoming a group member

One mention was made of Philip as part of the group, but if we think of the group as a learning community, including the adults, then Philip was a group member engaging in a kind of 'dance' with the adults. He came up with ideas and made a move; the adult responded with encouragement and kept him safe; he responded by being extremely pleased with himself and then made his next move.

Initiating and orchestrating projects

Philip's 'project' was learning to use both slides in as many different ways as he could. He was very good at initiating and carrying through his actions, even to the point of 'evading control'.

Asking questions

Although Philip did not use any expressive language during this sequence, I am sure that his body language indicated when he might, for example, ask for help. At 21 months, when he 'stepped a bit over the top' and the adult helped him get 'his second leg over without getting caught', his body language may have been questioning: What do I do now? or Can you help? or How do I do this? Also, when Philip 'sat poised at the top', he may have been inviting the adult to acknowledge his achievements. Carr *et al.* (2009: 119) state that, 'We ask questions in response to uncertainty and curiosity and indignation.' In this case Philip may have felt uncertain but also curious about how to get his body on to the top of the slide.

Exploring possible worlds

I think Philip was exploring a world where he could master the two slides. He was full of ideas, which, at his age, he put straight into action. We do not really know what he was thinking, but everything he did indicated exploration of the slides and of his body on the slides.

Storying selves

Again, without expressive language, we do not know what Philip was thinking, but repeating sequences of action connects with stories and storying. Philip was constructing and repeating a little story by repeating his actions. When he first came down the slide and tried to climb back up, he did this spontaneously. Gradually, he learned that he needed to carry out a set of actions: going up the steps; being on top; sliding down.

Using 'play' as a framework to understand

If we use Piaget's idea that play happens only when there is 'a predominance of assimilation' (1951: 150), then there is evidence of assimilation predominating on three occasions in these sequences.

1   At 22 months, when Philip 'turned himself over on the outdoor slide and went down on his stomach, feet first', and we are told he has already been encouraged to use this method on the indoor slide, we can infer that he is using this as practice and that he is assimilating fresh content (the outdoor slide) into a current pattern of coming down.

2   At 22 months, when Philip got to the stage of repeating his actions on the indoor slide sitting upright. We can assume that he has accommodated his actions to the very steep angle and that he is repeating his actions to practise.

3   At 22 months, when he 'sat poised at the top', he seemed to be relish-
ing the feeling of being on top for its own sake and, therefore, he was
assimilating rather than accommodating to getting himself into that
position as he was earlier.

Vygotsky's theory that play leads development would result in a slightly different reading of the situation. Whenever we observe a child working within their
zpd, his idea is that the play leads development.

At 21 months, Philip went to the top of the slide without a great deal of
awareness of how to get himself into a position to slide down. With help, he
managed to do that and it could therefore be argued that his wish to do what
other children were doing, i.e. going down the slide, resulted in him being able
to slide down. So the play of sliding down led his development of the ability to
slide down.

At 22 months, Philip used his experience of sliding down the outdoor
slide sitting up to lead the development of sliding down the much steeper
indoor slide sitting up. With practice, the wish and motivation to do this led
to the development of his skill to be able 'to keep the upright position for part
of the time'.

Winnicott's ideas on play are about the therapeutic nature of play and the
fact that play begins in the space between mother and baby. We can infer from
Philip's demeanour and enthusiasm that he entered nursery trusting and confident, and able to explore the environment. He expects adults to support his
explorations, which infers that he has been supported by his immediate family
from babyhood. He is able to take risks and to persevere in order to learn. He
is interested in physically seeing the world from different perspectives, i.e.
'on top of the slide' and 'facing out and backing down'. These explorations
will contribute to his ability to see things from different perspectives in his
thinking and feeling.

If we consider Philip's play in relation to Bruce's '12 features of free-flow
play' (2004: 149), we can pick out the relevant features that apply (the features
are underlined below and followed by a discussion of each).

One: in their play children use the first-hand experiences they have had
in life. In 'Philip and the Slide', Philip is 'learning directly through his senses'
(Bruce, 2004: 150). We can infer that he is building on other first-hand experiences he has had at home or out with his parents. The likelihood is that he has
used stairs at home so the steps he is attracted to are similar. The provision in
this setting for children under 3 is outstanding, and Philip takes full advantage
of the opportunities to master both the indoor and outdoor slides with support
at first.

Two: play does not conform to pressures to conform to external rules, outcomes, purposes or directions; because of this, children keep control of their
lives in their play. Philip is the initiator of his play. No mention is made of rules
to which he has to adhere. He appears to have complete freedom to try out his

own ideas. Therefore he can be an autonomous decision maker, which helps him keep control of his life.

Three: play is a process. It has no products. When the play ends, it vanishes as quickly as it arrived. Philip's actions on both slides have no product. Unless the actions are photographed, they vanish completely, they are here and gone.

Four: children choose to play. It is intrinsically motivated. It arises when the conditions are conducive, spontaneous, and it is sustained as it flows. Philip certainly chooses and is intrinsically motivated to carry out the actions described in these observations. His sheer pleasure in being on top and in sliding down, even when it is risky, is evidence of his intrinsic motivation. The setting, the equipment and the pedagogy, together with his natural exuberance, are all conducive to play.

Five: children rehearse the future in their play. Play helps children to learn to function, in advance of what they can do in the present. (This is similar to what Vygotsky believed.) I was not sure whether there was evidence of Philip rehearsing his future in this sequence of actions, as I tend to think of this in terms of pretend play and there was no evidence of Philip pretending or of using one thing to stand for another. However, he did seem to be learning to function in advance of what he could do. He pushed the boundary of his own capability when he managed to go on the outdoor slide and an adult held him back 'so that the speed would not alarm him'. He also pushed that boundary when he came down the very steep indoor slide sitting.

Eight: children and/or adults can play together, in parallel (companionship play), associatively or cooperatively in pairs or groups. Philip's play did not seem to be 'solitary' (see feature 7) although he was not necessarily part of a group. At his age, he seemed to be driven to explore and occasionally to be influenced by the actions of others, but also needing adults to be aware of his explorations so that they could support him and keep him safe. I am not sure that 'in parallel', 'associatively' or 'cooperatively' describe the situation adequately. Very young children need adults to be interested in what they are doing. Matthews (2003: 110) suggests that adults should be 'a more experienced learner' and 'an intellectual guide and companion'. A more able other person, who is present but not leading, could be the role of the adult with a child of Philip's age.

Nine: play can be initiated by a child or an adult, but adults need to bear in mind that every player has his or her own personal play agenda (which he/she may be unaware of) and to respect this by not insisting that the adult agenda should dominate the play. There is no doubt that Philip initiated this play on each occasion and that the adults in his setting respected what he was choosing to do. They supported him by watching and sometimes holding him back when he might have been overwhelmed or frightened.

Ten: children's free-flow play is characterised by deep concentration, and it is difficult to distract them from their learning. Children at play wallow in their learning. Concentration is sometimes associated with actions that are considered more cerebral or intellectual. Concentrating on the next actions I will try out on a slide seem rather different but valid when considering Philip's age. Philip was certainly practising in order to become more competent on both slides. I am not sure about whether he got to the point of wallowing in his learning in the observations considered but I do get the feeling that the wallowing would follow.

Eleven: in play children try out their recent learning, mastery, competencies and skills, and consolidate them. They use their technical prowess and confidently apply their learning. Philip continues to try out new ways of interacting with both slides, but also practises what he has recently tried out or achieved. An example is that he managed to descend the indoor slide (which was very steep) 'sitting up', and 'He repeated several times and was able to keep the upright position for part of the time'. This shows that he was trying out his recent learning in order to consolidate it.

So we can claim that nine features of free-flow play were apparent in these observations of Philip. According to Bruce, 'When seven or more features are present during play, we are likely to see effective learning' (2004: 149). We could see Philip learning during this sequence of observations.

Using a curriculum framework as a conceptual framework to understand

It could be quite illuminating to consider the observations of Philip in relation to the Early Years Outcomes (DfE, 2013) of the Early Years Foundation Stage (EYFS), which is the 'non-statutory guide to support practitioners' currently in use in England. The three primary areas are the focus for a report to parents between 2 and 3 years. These are 'Communication and Language', 'Physical Development', and 'Personal, Social and Emotional Development'.

In the observations being considered, most of the evidence is of 'Physical Development' and 'Personal, Social and Emotional Development'.

The difficulty with using statements about what children typically do is that the statements may not match up with what we are observing. In the case of Philip, he seems to be behaving in advance of his actual age in some ways.

With regard to the statements about 'physical development':

- At 22–36 months – 'Climbs confidently and is beginning to pull themselves up on nursery play climbing equipment' – Philip learned during the period of 20–22 months to climb up two very challenging pieces of equipment.
- At 30–50 months – 'Mounts stairs, steps or climbing equipment using alternate feet' – we do not know whether Philip used 'alternate feet', but we do know that he could mount steps and climbing equipment.

- At 40–60 months – 'Experiments with different ways of moving'. We certainly saw Philip moving on his tummy on the slide, sitting up on the slide, facing out and facing back when descending the steps. These are very different ways of moving.

With regard to the statements about 'personal, social and emotional development':

- At 22–36 months – 'Separates from main carer with support and encouragement from a familiar adult' – we saw in the contextual information that Philip was able to separate and to explore the environment in the setting. He was 'serene and undisturbed' when his mother left (Johnson, 1928/72: 170).
- At 22–36 months – 'Expresses his own preferences and interests' – this is apparent in Philip's actions.
- At 30–50 months – 'Can select and use activities and resources with help' – again, it is apparent that Philip is following his own interest in mastering the steps and slide.
- At 8–20 months – 'Interacts with others and explores new situations when supported by familiar person' – we can see that Philip is confident to explore the possibilities of both slides but also that he is supported, so that he does not get too frightened or hurt himself. We do not know how aware he is of the adult's support.
- At 16–26 months – 'Plays alongside others' – there is evidence that Philip joined the group who were walking up the indoor slide.
- At 22–36 months – 'Interested in others' play and starting to join in' – Again, going up the steps of the slide in the company of others suggests that Philip was interested in what other children were doing and beginning to join in.

So, we have seen that three observations of Philip that link together can be considered through five different conceptual frameworks in order to gain a deeper understanding.

Some questions to consider:

- What would enable you to gain a deeper understanding of children's actions?
- How might you take apart your observations?
- What do you want to learn about?
- What would you like to examine more closely?
- What would help you to consider children's learning?

Georgia and the trailer

Some context: Georgia started nursery a few weeks before this was filmed. She is playing outside with two friends she knows quite well. They are aware of being filmed.

A summary: Georgia (aged 3y 9m 2d) is interacting with two friends, pulling one, then the other, around in a trailer. When her friend gets out and climbs on a climbing frame, Georgia dashes to a post and secures the trailer. She quickly does the same with a second trailer. The three girls go over to the big slide and Georgia stands at the bottom of the slide expectantly.

The observation (4 minutes on video)

It is a bright, sunny autumn morning in the nursery garden. There are three children, two wooden trailers with long looped handles and two climbing frames outside. One of the trailers is oblong and big enough for a small child to lie down in. The other is much smaller. One climbing frame is square and the other is an 'A' frame. As I approach, Georgia is pulling the oblong trailer with Lana inside in an anti-clockwise direction around the 'A' frame. Georgia stops, Lana begins to climb out and tumbles on to the ground. Georgia looks uncertain and Lana comes over to tell me what has happened.

Georgia looks as though she is climbing in for a turn at being pulled, but climbs over the trailer and picks up the handle. Sam climbs in to the trailer, saying to Lana (and pointing), 'You have that one.' Georgia also points towards the other smaller trailer. Sam lies down in the first trailer. Georgia pulls it around 180 degrees, starts walking in the direction of the camera, then hesitates, looking towards the camera, before standing still, facing Sam and leaning the handle of the trailer on her hip ...

Georgia pulls the trailer around the square climbing frame in a clockwise direction. Lana runs after them saying something about 'going out on the minibus'. Sam leans out of the back of the trailer and says, 'I'm not going.' Georgia circles around the square frame pulling Sam in the trailer four times. She is working hard to pull the trailer with her friend inside and looks quite intent on continuing. She uses one hand but when the trailer gets caught on the frame on the third time around, she pauses to unhook it using both hands before continuing.

She starts to go around a fifth time. Sam points towards the gate and says something. Georgia shakes her head.

Sam climbs out of the trailer and on to the 'A' frame. Lana, too, climbs up the 'A' frame. G places the handle on the ground and goes towards the 'A' frame. Sam says something and points towards the gate again. Georgia returns to the trailer, picks up the handle, and walks quickly and purposefully towards the gate, looking down at the trailer behind her as she walks. She loops the handle of the trailer over a post, which is about chin high, and is near the gate. Georgia dashes over to show me what she has done. Lana comes over and looks. Georgia jumps and runs, saying, 'I'll put yours on there as well!' She dashes back to the 'A' frame and pulls Lana's trailer to the post, then struggles to hook the handle over, almost falling over as she manages to get the post through the looped handle. She is determined to loop both trailers on to the post and looks quite satisfied when the second trailer is secured.

The three children go over to the big garden slide and Georgia waits at the foot of the slide and holds her arms out when Sam slides down.

(Note: I have used pseudonyms for the two children Georgia is interacting with.)

Introducing the conceptual frameworks being used to analyse the observation of Georgia

Sometimes in a child observation study, it does not help to decide in advance which conceptual frameworks will offer insights into a child's learning. This piece of video is 20 years old now, but still available to be viewed, and we can still learn from watching it. When Georgia and I viewed this piece of video recently, we both felt that 'involvement' and 'well-being' would offer insights into Georgia's learning at that time (Laevers, 1997). In fact when we looked at all of the data, it was the emotional aspects that seemed most important. I felt that 'schemas' could also add insights into Georgia's developing interests.

'Involvement'

The concept of 'involvement', as explored by Laevers, is described in Chapter 4, so here is a quick reminder …

The signs of involvement are: 'concentration; energy; complexity and creativity; expression and posture; persistence; accuracy; reaction time;

language; satisfaction' (Laevers, 1997: 18). These signs are accompanied by a scale describing very low involvement (level 1) to extremely high involvement (level 5). When children are deeply involved in play, 'deep level learning' is taking place. In a more recent publication, Laevers and colleagues describe 'involvement' in the following way:

> Children with a high level of involvement are highly **concentrated and absorbed** by their activity. They **show interest, motivation** and even fascination. That is why they tend to **persevere** ... Their posture indicates **intense mental activity**. They fully experience sensations and meanings. A strong sense of **satisfaction** results from the fulfilment of their **exploratory drive** ...
>
> (2005: 10)

No one is deeply involved all of the time as they would burn out. When we assess 'involvement' we are not judging the child or their achievements in any way, but **we are looking at how well our provision matches their interests**. In Chapter 4, I question whether these signs might be extended for a child like Georgia, who never 'zones out' people. My conversation about 'involvement' with Georgia recently (aged 23y) is that she is aware of always knowing what the people around her are talking about and doing. So, consequently, she is never fully concentrating on what is in front of her, but her concentration spreads across what she is doing and hearing, and what people around her are doing.

'Well-being'

Alongside 'involvement' Laevers suggests that we also consider the emotional well-being of each child. Again Laevers offers the signs of well-being: 'openness and receptivity; flexibility; self-confidence and self-esteem; being able to defend oneself and assertiveness; vitality; relaxation and inner peace; enjoyment without restraints; being in close contact with one's inner self' (Laevers, 1997: 18–19). Alongside the signs of well-being, Laevers also provides descriptions ranging from very low well-being (level 1) to very high well-being (level 5). When a child's well-being is very high they are described as being like 'a fish in water'. They are confident, secure enough to explore and to make mistakes. They can be assertive and speak up for themselves, and they express their emotions appropriately. This means that, if they fall over and hurt themselves, we would expect them to cry. High well-being does not mean being happy at all times. **Anger and sadness can be expressed by children who have high well-being.** Emotional well-being can fluctuate during a day depending on the environment and what is happening. Changes affect and threaten children's well-being, especially if they are not handled well by the important people in their lives. However, children do not need to have perfect lives as they also need to build up resilience, so changes handled well can still be a challenge, but one that builds children's strength.

Schemas

Again, schema theory is introduced in Chapter 6, so this is just a brief reminder. Schemas are patterns of repeated actions, some of which result in marks, which can be up/down, side to side, round and round or dabs. Athey (2007: 62) divided marks into *'straight line* and *curves'*, and sub-divided them into 'twenty-four marks that were distinguishable from each other' (2007: 62). Bearing in mind that Piaget and Athey supported the idea that our actions become our thoughts, the making of marks with meaning is significant and usually fairly common by the age of 3 years. Athey (2007: 62) noted that, 'there is a correspondence or an equivalence between a graphic schema (*grid, core-and-radial, zig-zag lines, circles and semi-circles*) and experienced environmental content'.

In other words, children represent content they have experienced, often with a form (or schema) they are fascinated by.

'Georgia and the Trailer': an analysis

Involvement

With the benefit of having watched this several times, I can confidently pick out when I think Georgia was most involved. I have used a written transcript to mark up when Georgia was most involved and how involved I thought she was throughout. This process could be done with more rigour by two or more people. If you are part of a staff team, then discussing a child's involvement when you can watch a piece of video together results in a more reliable judgement being made. Similarly, watching alongside the child's parents gives you a more accurate sense of the child and their involvement.

Georgia was already 'engaged' with pulling the large trailer with Lana inside when I approached. The weight of the trailer with the child inside meant that Georgia had to 'concentrate' and use 'energy' to pull it and negotiate her way around the 'A' frame.

When Sam got in to the trailer, Georgia again had to 'concentrate', and use her physical strength and 'energy' to negotiate the trailer with a heavier child inside. She chose to turn the whole trailer around in order to move in the opposite direction. It could be argued that this involved effort and 'accuracy', although still on a large scale.

I was intrigued by Georgia standing still and leaning the handle of the trailer on her hip. She was certainly still involved but not in the same energetic way. Maybe she was 'reflecting' before moving on as she did soon after.

Georgia used a lot of 'energy' and seemed intent on continuing this journey around the square frame. When it got caught on the frame, Georgia had to show a little 'persistence' to solve the problem, which she did quite quickly by using two hands.

Georgia was most involved when she walked quickly and purposefully towards the gate. I do not know whether this looping over was something she had done before or whether she saw the possibility of anchoring the trailer to the post and this excited her. Georgia was extremely 'motivated' to carry out the same action with the smaller trailer and, after a bit of a struggle, when she had to show some 'determination', she managed to loop the second handle over and this was when she looked most 'satisfied'.

However, her ultimate purpose seemed to be to interact with the other two girls, particularly Sam. So she left what she had just done and went over to the slide to continue developing the play together. I think the relationships tested the 'limits of her capability' in a way that the physical actions did not (Laevers, 2005: 10). Georgia's main purpose was to interact with her friends, and this is what she was practising and trying out. Through her interest in relationships and in other people, Georgia has become very knowledgeable and adept at handling and maintaining relationships as an adult.

Well-being

In this observation, Georgia has recently started attending nursery and has had a two-week settling-in process when a close member of the family stayed with her. Starting nursery is a change, but it has been well handled and, on this occasion, Georgia gains security from playing with the children she already knows and from my presence as her grandmother. So her general well-being seems fairly high.

Georgia looked a bit 'uncertain' when Lana fell out of the trailer, and came to tell me what happened. We can only guess that Georgia felt that she might be blamed as she was in charge of the trailer. This little incident dampened her enthusiasm momentarily.

Georgia looked as though she was climbing into the trailer so may have been a bit uncertain about what to do next. Sam seemed to take control at this point and told Lana to have the smaller trailer. Georgia joined in agreement and seemed to regain her 'confidence' by being with Sam and agreeing with her. It is always tricky when three children play together and two of them pair up. Lana did not appear to be thrown at all by this and continued to join in the game pulling the smaller trailer behind her.

Sam again took control by saying she was not going out on the minibus, which meant that Georgia could continue with the game she was enjoying.

Georgia's well-being was high when she was problem solving (unhooking the trailer from the frame and looping the handles over the post). She gained some satisfaction and 'confidence' from being able to do this, while the other two girls were together on the 'A' frame. Georgia ran over to the big slide looking very 'open' to what would happen next but possibly hoping to interact some more with Sam.

Schemas

The effort Georgia was putting into pulling Lana around at the start of this observation suggested to me that Georgia might be interested in 'transporting'.

The fact that she went around the frame meant she was repeatedly 'going around' or 'enclosing' during her short journeys. She changed direction when she began to pull Sam around and she also switched to 'going around' the larger frame. We do not know why she made those two decisions, but they introduced variety into the content she was assimilating into her 'transporting' and 'enclosing' schemas.

When Georgia stood still and leaned the handle of the trailer on her hip, I think she was looking at the 'oblique trajectory' made by the handle. This was the 'figurative' aspect of the 'trajectory' schema.

Georgia pulled Sam in the trailer 'around' the square frame four times and would have done more. She was experiencing the weight, the direction in which she needed to travel and the force she had to use to make the trailer move.

Georgia was most excited at the prospect of the post 'going through' the handle in order to park or anchor the trailer near the gate. She also looked down at the trailer as she walked towards the gate. Again, the 'position' of the handle may have been of interest to her. Georgia was highly motivated to repeat the 'going through' action with Lana's trailer.

Finally, Georgia waited at the bottom of the slide for her friends to slide down. Again, she was possibly interested in the 'oblique trajectory', leading to an interest in angles and speed.

It may also be worth mentioning that there is a sort of 'pecking order' among these three girls, which is a sort of 'trajectory' or 'line' in their thinking, and evidenced by who makes decisions and who joins or follows. On this occasion, Sam seems to decide what will happen. Georgia is quite keen to follow her lead and Lana is complying with what the other two girls want to happen. However, this 'pecking order' shifts depending on who asserts themselves. Another 'trajectory', or 'line', which, on this occasion, is in line with the pecking order, is their ages, Sam being the eldest, Georgia in the middle and Lana the youngest. This is an immoveable line, although Georgia would like to be '4 before Sam', and frequently challenges and questions why this is the case.

After reading this observation and analysis of Georgia ...

- Which framework was most helpful to you in understanding Georgia?
- Would 'involvement' and 'well-being' be concepts you could use? (You may already be using them as their use is widespread in the UK now.)
- Are there any actions you would carry out as a result of knowing more about Georgia?

Issues to consider

- Am I getting a sense of how detailed my observations need to be?
- Which conceptual frameworks helped to deepen my understanding?
- How can I find out more about the frameworks I intend using?
- How can I ensure that my judgements are accurate?

8 An observational study of Georgia

> While such close, patient observation is rare in most teachers, it comes more easily to parents because of their interest in, and love for, their children. Like a naturalist, an observant parent will be alert both to small clues and to large patterns of behaviour. By noticing these, a parent can often offer appropriate suggestions and experiences, and also learn whether the help and explanations already given have been adequate.
>
> (Holt, 1989: 133)

The above quote from John Holt resonates with me as, whenever I have carried out a child study, I learn most from the parents and from the children themselves. The data provided by Georgia's parents, Ian and Colette, was more consistently gathered and showed more depth than anything that came from the nursery, the research study or the grandparents.

Introduction

This chapter brings together Georgia's story into a coherent whole, drawing on aspects from throughout the book. The purpose of this is to demonstrate how observations gathered over time can form a coherent whole and can demonstrate learning.

We gathered data about Georgia over more than three years. However, in order to more closely replicate what degree participants, practitioners or parents might do for a course, or just to get started on child study, I have selected data from Georgia's first few weeks at nursery. The data drawn on is from 5 September when Georgia was 3y 7m 10d, until 15 November, when

Georgia was 3y 9m 20d. I use square brackets to make comments related to what you may be required to do for an observational study.

Introducing Georgia

Georgia is the older child of Ian and Colette. She was aged 3y 7m 10d at the beginning of this short study. It begins with her first day at nursery. Her brother, Harry, is 15 months 23 days. Georgia lives with both parents and her younger brother in a small circular close of ten houses, all facing inwards. Georgia is one of the younger children in the close. There are seven girls older than Georgia and a boy and girl a bit younger as well as her younger brother. No one has moved in to or out of the close for some years. Georgia knows everyone in the close really well.

I am Georgia's maternal grandmother (known as 'Mop' to my grand-children) and I also work in the nursery Georgia is just beginning to attend for four mornings a week. Georgia's parents have used centre services since she was a baby, including baby massage, drop-in, playgroup and family room (a drop-in service for families).

Ethics

I gained initial written permission for this study of Georgia from her parents. They agreed to keep a diary of anything 'curious or interesting' Georgia did at home during the study period. I also talked with Georgia about her being part of my study. I continue to check with her that she is willing to be observed on each occasion. Georgia likes being the focus of a study and often requests that I 'write things down' that she has done. I have had meetings with Georgia's parents to share and to discuss the observations gathered. Together we try to interpret what is going on for Georgia.

[I am not anonymising Georgia or the setting in this study, as she is my granddaughter who already has a published book about her, and the setting in which I have worked for the last 25 years is well known to people in the early years field, so difficult to anonymise. Sometimes anonymity is a requirement for university courses.]

Method

This is an observational study using naturalistic methods, which means obser-vations are made in the normal course of events. No experimental situations are set up in order to 'test' responses in any way.

Mostly narrative handwritten observations were made using pen and paper, recording any language and actions. In addition, photos were taken and one four-minute sequence of video (described in detail in Chapter 7). A sample of the marks made by Georgia during this period was saved.

Georgia's 'Celebration of Achievements' folder from nursery offers information about her settling in to nursery and her initial explorations. The nursery workers make each child the focus of their written observations about every six weeks, so that they can plan for their learning as an individual. Georgia was the focus of observation at nursery twice during this period of study.

Georgia's parents wrote in a diary most days. I kept a diary at home on the days I saw Georgia outside of nursery. I also kept a research diary in order to reflect on what I had seen of Georgia's play and explorations, mostly at nursery.

The main purpose of the study is to understand Georgia's development and learning, and to be better able to build on home experiences at nursery.

Conceptual frameworks used to interpret the information gathered

In this short study I will be applying the following conceptual frameworks to the data, chosen on the basis of what seems most relevant for the data being considered. Also, these frameworks are often used by degree participants to make sense of their data in academic child observation studies:

- attachment theory and emotional well-being
- involvement
- schemas.

Attachment theory and emotional well-being

Observing Georgia as she begins to attend nursery inevitably involves considering how secure she feels in this new environment to explore freely. Starting nursery was not the only change for Georgia to cope with at this time. Her father had recently changed jobs and her mother starts working evenings during these first few weeks Georgia is attending nursery.

Bowlby defined 'attachment behaviour' as 'seeking and maintaining proximity to another individual' (Bowlby, 1997: 195). Bowlby observed that young animals and humans very quickly (within weeks of birth) 'recognised their primary caregiver', and that this 'preference was extremely strong and persistent' (1997: 196). Of all the species, the human baby is most dependent and 'for some months the infant is kept in proximity to the mother only by the mother's own actions' (1997: 199). By 3 months of age, a baby 'already responds differently to the mother as compared to other people' (1997: 199). Bowlby noticed that 'Proximity-maintaining behaviour is seen at its most obvious when mother leaves the room and the infant cries or cries and attempts to follow her' (1997: 200).

He also reported that there are changes with age. Significantly, for this study, Bowlby reported that it was usually around the end of the third year when 'most children become increasingly able in a strange place to feel secure with subordinate attachment figures' (1997: 205). Bowlby emphasised that there was wide variation in these average ages. So it is no coincidence that, in this country, for many years, we have seen starting nursery at around 3 years of age to be beneficial and not too traumatic for children.

Bowlby's research, along with the Robertsons' films of separations, have contributed to workers and parents thinking much more carefully about how to prepare for and handle separations for young children. (James and Joyce Robertson filmed children separated from their parents between 1948 and 1952, and followed them up in the 1960s. Viewers can see firsthand the distress experienced by young children during separation when no consistent person is available for comfort.) For example, Georgia's parents talked with her about starting nursery, for several weeks beforehand. Her Family Worker, Alison, visited Georgia and her family at home to see her in her own environment and to help Georgia make a relationship with her. Georgia also popped in to see Alison at nursery a couple of times before her start date. Most importantly, there was a two-week settling-in period when one of Georgia's important adults stayed within the nursery environment so that she could move away to explore in her own time.

Laevers' concept of 'well-being' is a 'process-oriented approach' that considers how a child is with regard to the signs of 'enjoyment', 'relaxation', 'vitality', 'openness', 'self confidence' and 'being in touch with their own feelings' (Laevers *et al.*, 2005: 7). The signs are accompanied by a scale going from very low well-being (level 1) to extremely high well-being (level 5). Being as relaxed and open in a new environment as in a familiar environment usually takes some time. Also 'well-being' can fluctuate from day to day, or even during a day. When children are tired, they can become overwhelmed and much less open and flexible. We see this inflexibility in the observations of Georgia at times.

We also see Georgia cling to those children and adults she already knows in this new environment. We understand that she clings in order to feel secure and that she moves away to explore or to get to know new children and adults when she is feeling secure.

Winnicott identified that young children often use 'transitional objects' to provide them with comfort when they are tired or distressed. Very young infants often adopt soft toys, blankets or thumbs as 'transitional objects' (Winnicott, 1991: 8). Georgia adopted Nancy, a soft doll, as a comfort object, and also a dummy, so her comfort at sleep times or when she was distressed were 'dummy and Nancy'.

Bruce came up with the idea that some children use 'objects of transition' to help them move from home to nursery and to connect the two (Bruce, 2004: 140). For this purpose, children use different objects, which are less personal and precious but do help with transitions from one place to another.

Involvement

Laevers and his team, in using a 'process-oriented approach', consider each child's 'involvement' alongside their emotional well-being. They describe the signs of involvement as 'motivation', 'intense mental activity', 'satisfaction', 'using one's exploratory drive' and working 'at the limits of your capabilities' (Laevers *et al.*, 2005: 10). Along with observing or looking out for signs of involvement, Laevers' team assess the level of involvement, going from 'uninvolved' at level 1 to 'highly involved' at level 5. As discussed earlier in this book, we are not judging a child's achievements or capability, but **we are judging how well the provision matches the child's interests**.

If a child's well-being is fairly high and they are becoming deeply involved in play some of the time, then we can deduce that they are engaging in 'deep level learning' (2005: 10).

Schemas

Schemas are repeated patterns of action that young children use in order to make sense of their worlds. Children try out their actions on different objects in order to find out what will happen and to generalise, for example, about what they can throw, carry, go around, go through and connect.

Children explore schemas in different ways (see Chapter 6 for a full explanation):

- through their actions
- through symbols, such as pretend play, marks, language – for example, after making friendship bracelets and playing with watches and various materials that go around, Georgia talked about something 'going around my waist'; at this point she was beginning to understand the concept of 'going around' and could use language appropriately as a symbol of the action
- through functional dependency relationships – for example, the trailer being anchored is functionally dependent on Georgia putting the loop 'around' the post (see Chapter 7)
- through thinking – for example, Georgia was trying to order events into a 'line' in her thinking and repeatedly asked, 'Why is Sam 4 before me?' (Sam would be 4 in November and Georgia would be 4 in the following January).

In this chapter, I will be talking about Georgia's exploration of:

- enclosing schema – enclosing oneself, an object or space
- trajectory/line schema – moving in or representing straight lines, arcs or curves

- connecting schema – children become interested in connecting themselves to objects and objects to one another (this also is apparent
emotionally).

The observations

The data gathered during this period has been summarised and placed on a
matrix showing 'the event', Georgia's exact age in years, months and days, and
the source of the information.

[Depending on your maximum word count, you may want to place a
matrix (like the one shown here as Table 8.1) in your Appendix and just refer
to it in the main body of your work. The matrix helps you make links between
events and informs the reader about the data on which you are drawing. As
well as written accounts, you could include transcribed conversations with
parents.]

A set of observations that tell us about Georgia's emotional well-being in the first few days of nursery

'Georgia (3:7:10) started nursery today – she's been looking forward to it. She
has also been refusing to go to crèche for the last couple of weeks – I think it's
all the changes that are happening.' (Parent)

'Georgia (3:7:11) ran in (to nursery) – was thrilled with a postcard from
Aunty Eloise. She put it into her box – said to me 'Want me a show you my box?'
(Grandparents)

'Georgia (3:7:13) drove me mad at nursery today – I felt like she was
really clingy both to me and Mop – she didn't want me to leave her at all.'
(Parent)

After the two weeks settling-in, the nursery produced information for
parents:

What Georgia did as soon as you left: *went straight to the rocking-horse*

What Georgia really enjoyed: *being in the snack area, loves stories and
picking the stories. Likes being close to adults*

Who Georgia spent time with: *Cath (Mop), Lynn (adult who does snacks
and is a friend of her mum's) and playing with Sam (a friend she knew
already)*

What Georgia ate: *cereal and crackers*

What Georgia found a bit difficult at first: *not having Cath or mum around
but settled in the snack area with Lynn*

Analysis

Georgia's well-being in these early days seemed to allow her to become
involved only when she was near to familiar adults.

Table 8.1 Matrix showing observations recorded in chronological order from Georgia was 3y 7m 10d until she was 3y 9m 20d

Event	Age	Data source
First day at nursery. Been refusing to go to crèche	3:7:10	Parent Diary
Nursery: Letter from Eloise in box/Playing with Craig 'Is he 4?' Distance jumping/Chose to go to Craig's group	3:7:11	Grandparents
Very clingy at nursery to Mum and Mop (grandmother)	3:7:13	Parent
Jumping off step/raffle tickets/big yellow bike/computer	3:7:14	Research
Went swimming with Uncle Paul 'I can swim by myself'	3:7:16	Parent &
Grandparents: Looking at prints and photos/Painting/'Gonna make a bracelet'		Grandparents
Played at home with raffle ticket book/needed one each. Played with sellotape involved in how to hold. Still into why friend is 4 before her	3:7:17	Parent
Dice, woodwork and friendship with Craig	3:7:18	Nursery
Remote control car disappearing and appearing/hand drill and wood at nursery/Interest in size and fit	3:7:19	Parent
Weekend in Bournemouth/no floor under water/asked for stabilisers off	3:7:22	Parent &
At nursery painting/conversation with mum about not being very involved		Research
Sellotape on paper/Jumping to reach/Obsessed with time	3:7:24	Parent
Home: Trying to tie shoelaces/Size of friendship bracelets	3:7:25	Parent &
Nursery: Gluing and painting around edge of paper first		Research
Gluing/Drying and peeling/Trying to ride without stabilisers. Playing 'Farmer's in his Den' and showing brother 'Ring-a-Roses'	3:7:26	Parent
Wore friend's braces while looking at catalogue/Wants Daddy to take her to Wicksteed and the pub/Playing rough physical game with children in close	3:7:28	Parent

(Continued)

Table 8.1 (Continued)

Event	Age	Data source
Grandparents: Gluing around edge – space in middle for name and date/Identifying letters in her name/Interested in time and number/Negotiated time to stay til/Wants to know who can drive nursery minibus/Knows who is in which group at nursery/Sang 'Ring-a-rosies'/Interested in streetlights/Wants to be 4 and a half	3:7:29	Grandparents
Home: Conversation with mum about her age	3:8	Parent & Research
Nursery: Helped with photocopying – surprised we have 2 photocopiers		
Home: Can ride 2 wheeler/Material around leg – fit?/Language 'around my waist'/Put on watch	3:8:1	Parent & Nursery
Nursery: Woodwork then workshop		
Pushing buggy, trolley/Playing 'Mummies, Daddies and Babies'/Not letting friend out of room/Batteries 'look new'	3:8:2	Parent
Wants to go to church	3:8:3	Research
Home: Knows Asda is near Nanny's and Safeway near home	3:8:5	Parent & Research
Nursery: Playing 'driving to Scotland' with friend in toy car		
Home: Went to church and Georgia was bored	3:8:6	Parent & Research
Nursery: Looking for security and sussing out rules		
Nursery: With Mop and Leon riding bikes then involved gluing for 20m with friend	3:8:8	Research
Home: Asked Dad 'You looking at ingredients?' on way home knew hotel on right	3:8:10	Parent, Nursery & Research
Nursery: Swapping shoes with friend/Building/Stories 'Avocado Baby' and 'Angry Arthur' Rivalry and possessiveness		
Home: 'Why don't we call the Evs the darms?' (Everard Arms)	3:8:11	Parent
'Where's Wally' several times/Time and distance/Cut paper into strips and joined together around my wrist/ Fastening and unfastening my watch/Wants a watch	3:8:12	Grandparents
Puzzle – How can I hear Harry when I am holding phone in my house?	3:8:13	Grandparents

Table 8.1 (Continued)

Event	Age	Data source
Played on computer at nursery and demanded 5 copies/Very interested in holding babies	3:8:14	Parent
Home: Georgia and friend play with string around each other like reins	3:8:15	Parent & Research
Nursery: Could see moon/Timing turn on bike/Went to Howitts with Mop and Leon		
Home: Aware of mum observing/Playing with colour pegs (categorising?)	3:8:16	Parent
Nursery: Georgia wore Mop's watch (for time away and security)	3:8:18	Research
Grandparents: Played with Mah-jong counting and recognising symbols/Played on computer typing and deleting/Had 'Papa please get me the moon' x2	3:8:21	Grandparents & Research
Nursery: Atlas and Liam/Guess Craig lived at Danesholme (he didn't)		
Nursery: Carried around conkers/Estimating and counting/Size of shoes	3:8:24	Research
Brought conkers on string from home/Wore one around her neck	3:8:25	Research
Went to interactive science display/Bought Georgia 'I want my teddy' – she was going to put it into the bin but loved it when we read it. Saw rainbow	3:8:26	Grandparents
Home: Wants mum to write that 'she is playing with conkers and on her bike'/Also sings rude songs	3:8:28	Parent
Home: Makes circle of coins and counts – forgets where she started	3:8:29	Parent
Nursery: Computer	3:8:30	Research
Home: At friend's house – writes dad's name – uses 3 symbols	3:9	Parent, Nursery & Grandparents
Nursery: Asks Mop 'write about me – what you do at Pen Green'		
Grandparents babysitting: Both children tired and upset. Georgia tore up her writing/Comforted by having dummy and Nancy/Said I couldn't come to her party or the zoo/Played cards with Pop and can match suits/Interested in duration '3 weeks' searched for equivalent, i.e. 'friend's holiday?'		

(Continued)

Table 8.1 (Continued)

Event	Age	Data source
Trip to East Carlton/Notices the moon is out/Can fasten badge/Brought popper to nursery	3:9:1	Nursery
Nursery: Georgia and the trailer (filmed sequence)/Asked for Farmer's in the Den	3:9:2	Research
Home: Holding book in different positions while mum in bath	3:9:3	Parent
Home: 'do I look like a Frenchman?' (collar up)	3:9:4	Parent &
Went to zoo/Georgia loved it all/In car talked about 'a barrowful of apples', 'a frog in my throat' and 'ants in my pants'		Grandparents
Home: Interested in the Lidl shop and wants to know why cars there if not open	3:9:6	Parent &
Nursery: Pulling friend and being pulled in trailer up slope/Pretending to go to fireworks/Watched other children having foot massage/Rolling play dough and listening/Pretending to be the baby with two friends/ Pedalling around on bike/At gym throwing balloons in air/Watching others on slide and then going on slide		Nursery
At garage: Why one car is higher?/Questions about moon being out/Cut paper into small pieces and gathered up	3:9:7	Grandparents
Family Room: Deduction – Weetabix here, therefore Ellen must live here	3:9:8	Parent
Home: Holding up different 3s/Counting so she's always number 5	3:9:9	Parent &
Stories/Sizes and categorising boys' things and girls' things/Are my feet bigger because I am older?/Fitting cupboard in car		Grandparents
Home: Tummy rumbled – 'farting in my tummy'	3:9:10	Parent
Home: Friends 'desperate' to see my new shirt	3:9:11	Parent
I HAD BEEN OFF FOR A WEEK	3:9:12	Research
Nursery: Georgia is wearing friend's 4 year old badges/Massaging her friend's feet/Called me 'Cath'		
Nursery: Thought she'd lost her friend's party invitation	3:9:13	Research

Table 8.1 (Continued)

Event	Age	Data source
Home: Played with mum's jewellery box, buttons and bags/Experimenting with crayons and damp cloth	3:9:14	Parent
Home: 'Mine scorp needs to be 10' on computer – knows 3 is much lower than 10 and 10 is the highest	3:9:15	Parent,
Nursery: Hopping and nail varnish important/Upset at soft room		Research &
Distance hopping/What time is story? Who is target child? Recognised her name/Heard Elephant and the bad Baby		Nursery
Home: Talking about going to London 'to see the Queen'	3:9:16	Parent &
Nursery: Shouted 'Cath' when she saw me		Research
Home: Duration of staying up – what's more?	3:9:17	Parent &
Had Alfie story/Sulked because no cheese spread/Looked at photos from massage/Massaged mum's feet/ Had torn up pic and left in car/Mum suggested repairing it with sellotape – Georgia agreed 'Yes with sellotape'		Grandparents
Home: Made a circle from 2 semi circles	3:9:18	Parent
Home: Talking about what will happen 'when she's 6' Says Daniel goes to 'old Lady's School' 'Tickled onions'	3:9:19	Parent,
Nursery: Not well settled today – Cath and Alison not in nursery		Research &
Nursery: Layering paint on paper		Nursery
Nursery: Demonstrating purple popper to other children/Massage 'Want me a do yours?'	3.9.20	Research &
Playing babies with Sam and Lana – Georgia was the baby		Nursery

Key to data sources:
Parent = Diary kept by parents of anything 'curious or interesting' Georgia did at home
Nursery = Celebration of Achievement from nursery using 'target' child system, i.e. each child observed every six weeks
Research = Reflective diary kept for research purposes
Grandparents = Diary kept by grandparents of any contact with Georgia

'Refusing to go to crèche' reveals her ambivalence towards what she knows well (crèche) and what is imminent (nursery). On the one hand, she is rejecting what she knows well in favour of the new experience but, at the same time, she is clinging on to those people she knows, for security in the new environment. The pressure felt by parents in these sorts of situations is very real. As workers, we can help by reassuring children and parents that new experiences need time to adjust to.

It was significant that she brought to nursery a postcard from her favourite Aunty Eloise and put it into her box, which was her private space at nursery to use for whatever she wished. She could go and look at the postcard and remind herself of times when she felt more relaxed and confident.

Strategies Georgia developed for feeling more secure and confident

Nursery was not the only new experience for Georgia around this time:

'We went to Bournemouth for the weekend to stay with friends. Georgia (3:7:22) had an excellent time – I hardly saw her. She spent most of the weekend playing outside on Carla's bike (with stabilisers). She had asked Mop to come and take her stabilisers off her bike while we were away.' (Parent)

Georgia may have been thinking about how the bike without stabilisers would feel when she said, while on a short boat trip:

'There's no floor under the water'

Mother: 'What do you think is under there?'

Georgia: 'Don't know' (Parent)

Just over a week later, her parents reported that, at home, 'Georgia (3:8:1) (age in years, months and days) can now ride her two wheeler herself. She's very proud of herself!' (Parent)

Another strand in Georgia's explorations was to know exactly how nursery worked.

At 3:7:29, at nursery Georgia knew I could drive the minibus and 'wanted me to do a trip on the nursery minibus to East Carlton or Wicksteed Park'. She was interested in which other adults could drive the minibus. 'I explained who can drive the minibus and why. She thought Marcus would be able to, also asked "Val is 55?" I think she meant 25 as I said you have to be 25 or over. Also talked about which child was in which group at nursery. She knew that Lana was in Val's group, Emma was in Lucy's group and Sam was in Val's group.' (Grandparents)

At 3:8:18, Georgia knew that I would always be attending a management meeting on a Monday morning: at nursery, 'Georgia wore my watch this morning. She understands I have a meeting on a Monday so am not in nursery.' (Research)

Analysis

Athey stated that 'competence increases confidence' (2005), and this certainly seemed to be the case for Georgia. Challenging herself to ride her bike without stabilisers was a significant step and she seemed to be thinking about how it would feel (as though there was no floor underneath?). When she achieved it she felt proud of herself. Her well-being was high at this point.

Georgia needed to know where people were and what would happen in order to feel secure at nursery. She seemed to need to know how the whole system worked. Knowing I was going to a meeting every Monday prompted Georgia to borrow and wear my watch. She could not tell the time yet but she did have a notion about time. It was also probably to do with having something precious of mine to hold on to while I was not there. This could link with 'objects of transition' as described by Bruce (2004: 140).

Situations that resulted in low well-being for Georgia

Georgia was desperately trying to feel more powerful and in control at this time. Knowing about the nursery system and what would happen helped. Georgia was also trying to assert herself with her friends:

At 3:8:2, at home 'This afternoon Georgia and Lana were going upstairs to play "mummies, daddies and babies". After a while the door kept slamming and I could hear them arguing. I called up to Georgia to open the door and Lana immediately came down. Lana obviously did not want to play this game! A bit later Georgia told me "I wasn't letting Lana out of mine room cos I wanted her to play mummies and babies and she didn't want to."' (Parent)

At 3:8:10, at nursery: 'Georgia was doing some building. She seemed to be in competition with Lana and Sam, who were also building. She was saying to Lana, "You can't do this" (about a ramp Georgia had built) and was asking me to photograph hers. I photographed each of them and told Georgia they were all different and I liked them all. When Sam first arrived I said, "Oh you look nice" (she was wearing a dress). Georgia said, "I'm going to wear my dress tomorrow … and my petticoat", then added "it's got a big hole in it", and laughed. Georgia and Sam swapped shoes quite early and wore each other's all morning.' (Research)

At 3:9, at home when we were babysitting because her father was late home: 'Both children were tired and upset when Colette had gone. Georgia was really cross and upset – she tore up the writing she had done for me. She was distraught until she said she wanted dummy and Nancy, and I said that was fine. She said I could not go to her party and she did not want me to go to the zoo (this weekend). She said that Harry, mummy, Pop, Paul and Eloise could go to the zoo but she would lock me in the house by myself.' (Grandparents)

Analysis

Georgia was expressing her anger when others did not do what she wanted. She felt threatened and jealous when I gave attention to other children at nursery. It was hard for her having me at nursery with responsibility for other children. She needed to know that she was extra special to me. However, she did not lose her sense of humour, as shown in her comment 'It's got a big hole in it', probably said for the benefit of her friends.

At home, she was just very weary, expecting her father home and instead had me. She vented her anger on me in the only way she knew how: by telling me I could not come to her party or go to the zoo with the family that weekend.

What helped to raise Georgia's well-being

Georgia was very fond of stories and often chose stories in which emotional issues came up:

At 3:8:10, at nursery: 'Georgia chose "Avocado Baby" and "Angry Arthur" – both are stories she also has at home.' (Nursery) (Avocado Baby is about a baby that eats avocado, becomes incredibly strong and frightens away a burglar. Angry Arthur is about Arthur's uncontrollable anger.)

Role play with her friends also seemed to help Georgia see things from other perspectives. Twice, during these few weeks, 'Georgia pretended to be the baby' in games with Lana and Sam.

When Georgia was 3:9:12 I had been on holiday for a week so had not seen her at home or at nursery: 'I was at work only briefly today. Georgia was at nursery and wearing Sam's 4 year old badge and was massaging Sam's feet for a long time in the corridor. She shouted "Hi Cath" as I was leaving.' (Research)

At 3:9:17, at home: when Georgia could not have cheese spread 'went behind couch not speaking to anyone. Came out of sulk to show me recent photos of her and Harry at massage and subsequently to massage Colette's feet.' (Grandparents)

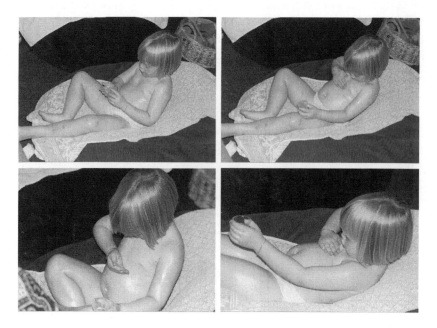

Figure 8.1 Georgia massaging herself

(The photos in Figure 8.1 were taken when Georgia was attending a massage session with her mother at their local centre for young children and families. In this instance, she was using the photos at home, to reflect on an experience. Georgia, as an adult, has given permission for these photos, and all of the others, to be included in this book.)

Later that same day at home: 'Colette suggested repairing a picture Georgia had torn up earlier. Colette said maybe they could fix it together. Georgia said "Yes, with sellotape."' (Grandparents)

Analysis

Georgia seemed to understand the emotional themes of the stories at some level. Expressing the wish to feel stronger and more powerful but also angry at times were themes she could identify with. The articulation of those feelings almost certainly helped.

Being a 'baby' in role play can be quite a powerful role. Babies do not have a great deal of responsibility but everyone listens and responds to them. We do not have in detail what happened in the role-play situations, but most young children use role play to explore and try out how to interact in real-life relationships.

The challenge of me being away from nursery for a week seemed to result in Georgia feeling much stronger and feeling more like the other children in relation to me. The fact that she called me by my first name, as other children did, was a sign of her being much more relaxed and at home in the nursery situation than previously.

Massage is soothing, and remembering the feeling by reflecting on the photos seemed to calm Georgia down and make her feel better. Repairing her torn picture with her mother's help also seemed to be understood at more than one level. Relationships, too, can be repaired and help is available.

Observations that tell us what Georgia began to be involved in during those first few weeks she was attending nursery

Georgia was frequently involved in talking about nursery and trying to work out how everything functioned, as described in the last section. There was certainly 'intense mental activity' whenever Georgia was puzzled or trying to find out about something through questioning adults (Laevers *et al.*, 2005: 10). These sorts of conversations were usually with her parents or grandparents at home, but occasionally at nursery – for example, 'Why is the moon out during the day?' (on a nursery trip).

At nursery: Georgia (aged 3:8:1) 'came over to the workbench. She hammered two wheels on to an oblong piece of wood. Fetched felt pens for me to put her name on, then represented her name herself. Sam gave her some stamps, which she tried to stick on the wood. I asked, "What would make them stick?" I offered to bring her glue but she noticed some paint on the workshop table and wanted to use that. She and her friend, Sam, took their woodwork to the workshop and worked alongside two other girls. Georgia painted the wood and then selected and cut off pieces of different materials to add. She left her creation with me to go to the toilet … I looked for her ten minutes later and she was on the computer and stayed there 'til storytime.'

Analysis

This observation encapsulates a lot of what Georgia was attracted to in nursery at this time. The woodwork bench was a novelty and not something she had access to at home, so trying out hammering and drilling was new to Georgia and something she was keen to explore. Another aspect was trying to write her name. She was at that 'in between stage', between pretend writing and recognising the symbols we all use. So recognising her name and trying to represent her name and Harry's name was still a challenge to her. At 3:7:25, Georgia produced the marks in Figure 8.2, showing an 'H' and an almost recognisable 'G'.

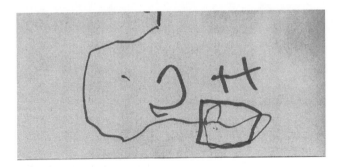

Figure 8.2 Georgia's mark making at 3:7:25

Similarly, the workshop provided more resources and lots more choices than she had at home. Georgia liked cutting and selecting bits to add on. In Figure 8.3 she is most involved in the workshop at nursery at 3:7:28.

Finally, it was no coincidence that Georgia did not return to the workshop, as her other favourite activity at this time at nursery was going on the computer.

Observations that help us identify the 'threads of thinking', or schemas, Georgia was exploring

Enclosing

The predominant pattern explored by Georgia during these few weeks was 'enclosing'. Examples include the following.

Figure 8.3 Georgia in the workshop at 3:7:28

At 3:7:16, at her grandparents': 'Did painting – used a bit of computer paper – tore off the bit with holes in – placed it on paper – painted one side, then turned it over and painted the other side. Said at one point "I'm gonna make a bracelet" (an "enclosure").'

At 3:7:25, at home: 'Georgia has been trying to tie shoelaces – she can do the first bit, make a loop and put the other lace around it, but can't quite get it through the hole …'. Later that day, 'Georgia came to me with a piece of embroidery thread and asked me to tie it around her wrist (like her friendship bracelets) – I did one and she then came back with another piece and said "You could tie this around my wrist if it's big enough." Her mum responded "It's not, it's too short, it won't fit around." Georgia replied "Anna could have it" (Anna is Georgia's doll). She then brought another bigger piece for her other wrist.' That same day at nursery, 'Georgia did gluing and painting – painted on round paper, all around the edge and then filled in the space in the middle' ('enclosing' the space before filling it in).

The following day, at 3:7:26, her parents reported that, at home, 'Georgia has been playing "The Farmer's in his Den" outside in the close with the girls and, this evening, she was showing Harry how to play "Ring-a-roses"!' ('going around' or 'enclosing' space in two different ring games).

In a video observation at 3:9:2, at nursery: we saw Georgia 'going around' or 'enclosing' a climbing frame pulling her friend in a trailer several times (see Chapter 7 for the full observation).

[If this were a study in which a short video observation was required, this four-minute clip would be suitable, along with the preceding examples of 'going around' or 'enclosing'.]

Analysis

All that summer the older girls in the close had been making friendship bracelets, so it is no coincidence that Georgia, too, wanted to make them. First, Georgia seemed to be recognising what could be turned into a bracelet. The edge of the computer paper was narrow and long with perforations at regular intervals. Although she did not actually make it into a bracelet, she could see that possibility, so she was 'thinking' about a line as an 'enclosure'.

Tying shoelaces involves 'going around' or 'enclosing' a space and 'going through', and is quite a complicated and coordinated set of actions. Georgia was just beginning to practise those actions. She could manage the 'going around' but not quite manage the 'going through' action.

She seems interested in estimating the size of 'line' needed to go around her wrist and when her mum told her it would not fit her wrist she immediately thought about it fitting a much smaller wrist – that of her doll, Anna.

Georgia chose round paper, although a variety of shapes were available, and painted 'around' the edge before filling in the space in the middle.

The ring games are another exploration of 'going around' or 'enclosing' space or a person. Also pulling her friend 'around' the climbing frame was another variation of that 'enclosing' action.

Trajectory

Another less obvious pattern was 'trajectory', or 'line', as observed in the following examples.

On Georgia's second day at nursery, at 3:7:11, 'Craig jumped from 2nd step to floor in low ceiling area. Georgia wanted to know "Is he 4?" I said that he is. Both spent a while jumping from 2nd step as far as they could.' (Grandparents)

At 3:7:16, at nursery: 'Georgia returned to jumping off step with Craig.' (Research)

At 3:7:24, at home: 'Georgia has been jumping up trying to reach things – still doing things with tip-toes and without. A couple of times she has also got inside a pillowcase and jumped about.' (Parent)

On the same day, at home: 'Georgia is still obsessed with time – how long it takes to get places – how long until something happens. Whether it is a long time or not.' (Parent) (This could be conceptualised as a 'line' or measure of time.)

At 3:8:5, at home: Georgia is beginning to use her 'trajectory' schema in her thinking when she has a conversation about the distance between Nanny's house and Asda, and the distance between Safeway and home. (Parent) (Another 'line' or journey that involves a measure of distance.) On the same day, Georgia plays 'driving to Scotland' at nursery with her friend. (Research)

At 3:9:15, at home: Georgia's parents report her frustration when the computer tells her that her score is 3 (on a game). 'Georgia: "That's wrong – my scorp needs to be 10!"' (Another 'line' from less to more.)

Analysis

Jumping as far as possible from the 2nd step was a very obvious example of exploring a 'trajectory' that links with distance. Georgia's question, 'Is he 4?', is a less obvious example of exploring a 'trajectory' to do with increasing age. Georgia knew that she was 3 and would be 4 on her next birthday. She was very interested in and trying to understand 'lived age' as a concept, so understanding whether Craig was her age or older was relevant. Age is a kind of measure of time from birth. Georgia was really struggling to understand why Sam would be 4 before her. She could not yet hold in mind the idea of different starting points – that is, Sam was born in November and Georgia in January. Georgia's perception was that they should both be 4 at the same time.

Jumping up to reach things is also connected with distance, but in the vertical plane this time. Reaching an object is functionally dependent on her jumping high enough, so this is an exploration of the functional dependency relationship between her action and reaching a certain point.

Time is another concept that can be conceptualised as a line. In this instance, Georgia is linking the journey travelled with how long it takes, so she is trying to coordinate two different trajectories in her thinking.

Georgia shows she can compare journeys, or 'trajectories', when she has a conversation about which supermarket is near Nanny's and which is near home. Of course, this knowing about distance is based on her many experiences of travelling those journeys and probably of hearing her parents make those sorts of comparisons. 'Driving to Scotland' in a toy car at nursery showed that Georgia was also exploring the 'trajectory' or journey symbolically.

Georgia's indignation at scoring only 3 on a computer game is evidence that she has some understanding of a 'line' from zero to 10 and that 3 is lower than 10.

Connecting

Staying close to those adults and children she already knows during those first few days at nursery are a form of 'connecting'. We stay connected to or with familiar people in order to feel safe and secure.

At 3:7:24, at home: 'Georgia has a roll of sellotape which she has really enjoyed playing with lately. She has been cutting off different length strips and sticking them randomly on to paper.' (Parent)

At 3:8, at home, having a conversation about her mum's age:

Georgia: 'You are eleventeen?'
Mum: 'No'

Georgia:	'Six?'
Mum:	'No'
Georgia:	'Twenty?'
Mum:	'No, I've been twenty'
Georgia:	'When were you twenty?'
Mum:	'Six years ago'
Georgia:	'That was one minute ago?'
Mum:	'No – six years ago'
Georgia:	'Six minutes ago?'
Mum:	'No six years ago'
Georgia:	'Twenty years ago?'
Mum:	'No six years ago'

... and other conversations about age (this involves estimating her mum's age and moving along or up and down a 'line' of increasing age).

At 3:8:1, at nursery: 'Hammered 2 wheels on to wood.' (Nursery)

At 3:8:8, at nursery: 'Left us to go and do some gluing in the workshop with Sam. She was very involved there for at least 20 minutes.' (Research)

Georgia also seems interested in the parts that 'connect' to make something whole – for example, at 3:8:10 at home, she asked her dad, when he was looking closely at a pot of fromage frais: 'You are looking to see if Harry's allowed that? You looking at ingredients?' (Ingredients are the parts that 'connect' to make up the whole fromage frais.)

The next day, her mother reports, 'We drive past the Everard Arms on the way to nursery in the morning. Georgia quite often asks the name of the pub and I've told her "The Everard Arms" or "The Evs" for short. Today she said "Why don't we call it 'the darms' – that would be good!"' ('The Evs' is one part and 'the darms' is the other part of the name – they 'connect' to make the name.)

At 3:8:12, at her grandparents: 'Georgia cut up paper into strips and joined them around my wrist (she might like bandaging). She fastened and unfastened my watch more precisely than on holiday a couple of months ago. Saying which hole is the right size and asking "Is it too tight?" Also asked to make a book – became very interested in undoing the sellotape, cutting with big scissors, hanging it on the edge of the table (very, very involved).' (Grandparents)

At 3:8:13, at home: Georgia was puzzled that when we were speaking by phone, I was in my house but could hear Harry crying in the background at her house. 'She said "But you're in your house." I said "But I'm holding the phone." She said "I'm holding the phone."' (Grandparents)

Analysis

Attachment theory, as well as schema theory, helps to explain why we need to stay near familiar people when we are in unfamiliar surroundings. At the very least, this is a survival mechanism. Trevarthen would argue that we also need to stay close for 'companionship' (2002). Trevarthen argues that very young children are trying to 'share meaning' and 'have fun' with those around them, so, in those terms, Georgia was enjoying sharing the new environment of nursery with those people she knew well, which was another reason for staying 'connected' to those people she knew already and could communicate with.

Using sellotape, hammering and gluing are all different ways to physically 'connect' materials together and easily recognised as having something in common.

The conversation about her mum's age did not immediately strike me as being about 'connecting', but when you look at Georgia's questions, she was desperately trying to 'connect' one idea with the next, and all in the abstract, so much more difficult for a young child.

The context in which Georgia lived provided information about allergies as Harry had a serious dairy allergy, so thinking about the ingredients that go together, or 'connect', to make up a product was apparent in her conversation with her dad.

The conversation about 'The Evs' was interesting, as it involved Georgia deconstructing or 'disconnecting' the words and being highly creative about how it could be shortened. She had some awareness of the parts (or syllables) that 'connect' to make up the whole name.

The observation where Georgia was 'connecting' in order to 'go around' my wrist shows a coordination of 'connecting' and 'enclosing', and an interest in the concept of 'size and fit'. When making a book, Georgia was much more interested in the process – for example, hanging the sellotape on the edge of the table, so that it stayed 'connected' and did not get tangled.

The final observation, when we were on the phone, demonstrates Georgia's puzzle to understand how I can hear what is happening in her house, although I am at home. We are 'connected' to each other and talking, but she does not yet seem able to picture what my experience is while we are talking. This is a complex set of ideas, requiring imagination and abstract thinking. The puzzle disequilibrates Georgia, and more experience and talking helps her to accommodate to the idea that I can hear what is going on in the background, while we are 'connected' by phone … but not during these few weeks.

Conclusions and implications for practice

The purpose of this short study was to understand Georgia's development and learning during her first few weeks at nursery. Her emotional well-being seemed to be most important. She needed to feel secure and in control, and she managed this by, first, interacting with people she already knew and, second, by understanding the whole system.

Georgia became involved in knowing more about aspects that were new to her, such as woodwork and the workshop environment, so novelty was a factor in her becoming involved.

Measuring time and space seemed to be at the forefront of some of Georgia's schematic explorations. Her firsthand experiences were important in being able to understand and to estimate, and these were experiences such as jumping, which she could feel through her whole body, and journeys in the car, along with conversations that helped her articulate her concerns.

The second purpose of this study was to build on home experiences at nursery and I think this was achieved in a broad way, by offering a workshop environment where Georgia could choose for most of the time at nursery. There are some direct links – for example, a conversation about going to East Carlton Park on the minibus and a nursery trip there with her family worker a few weeks later.

Practices like home visiting and daily chats about children's well-being and learning were, and continue to be, critical. Building trust and knowledge between key persons and families is a major part of working with young children. The implications for practice could also include parents sharing children's questions with nursery workers as these seemed to offer the deepest insights into Georgia's thinking and puzzles.

The conversations between the adults also resulted in her parents building on what Georgia enjoyed at nursery – for example, that Christmas, Georgia's main present was a trailer identical to the one she enjoyed using at nursery.

Concluding thoughts

> Chibi learnt from staring at ceilings, gazing out of windows, wandering the hills, and listening with great attention and interest to birds. But it wasn't until Mr. Isobe appeared in his sixth year of school that he found out he could also learn in school and that what he had learned out of school was important, valuable and of interest to others ... Mr. Isobe saw no clear distinction between teachers and learners ... (Goodman and Goodman, 1990: 226)
>
> We all learn from one another and never more than when we make an individual study of a child.

There are many ways of putting together or constructing a child observation case study. As it is basically the story of what happened for one child over time, putting everything into chronological order helps to give it the 'form' of a story with a beginning, middle and end. However, depending on the purpose of the study, certain features may need to be pulled together in different sections, and each of those would probably be in chronological order, rather than the whole. So please treat the following plan as a suggested step-by-step guide.

Step One: Think about the purpose of your study and any questions you want to address.

Step Two: Identify your principles and values (as a team).

Step Three: Think about your beliefs about how children learn, and choose a child to study.

Step Four: Gather information about the child's context, where they are in their family, their interests, family hobbies and experiences they have had.

Step Five: Consider ethics – how you go about your study deserves consideration all the way through the process, but particularly at the beginning when you think about how you will behave towards the participants, and how you will respect their views and wishes (see Chapter 2).

Step Six: Think about how you will carry out your observations and which tools and techniques to use, including the advantages and disadvantages (see Chapter 3).

Step Seven: Bearing in mind what you want to find out, make a plan about when and where you can gather the most useful information, remembering that the child's 'involvement' is key to making useful observations.

Step Eight: Make the observations and then make a summary matrix (as shown in the examples in Chapters 5 and 8). Select material to include by marking up your observations (useful techniques are described in Chapter 5).

Step Nine: Decide on the conceptual frameworks that you will use to illuminate learning (suggestions are in Chapters 6 and 7).

Step Ten: Apply the conceptual frameworks to your selected data, carry out your analysis, and draw conclusions and implications for practice. (It helps to step away from your story for a few days in order to think about how what you have found out will be shared, and can be applied to and will affect your practice.)

References

American Psychological Association (APA) (2010) *Ethical Principles of Psychologists and Code of Conduct*. Washington, DC: APA.

Arnold, C. (1990) Children who play together have similar schemas. Unpublished dissertation, Peterborough Regional College.

Arnold, C. (1997) Understanding young children and their contexts for learning and development: building on early experience. Unpublished MEd study, University of Leicester.

Arnold, C. (1999) *Child Development and Learning 2–5 years: Georgia's Story*. London: Sage.

Arnold, C. (2003) *Observing Harry: Child Development and Learning 0–5 years*. Maidenhead: Open University Press.

Arnold, C. (2014) Schemas: a way into a child's world. *Early Child Development and Care*, DOI: 10.1080/03004430.2014.952634.

Arnold, C. and the Pen Green Team (2010) *Understanding Schemas and Emotion in Early Childhood*. London: Sage.

Atherton, F. and Nutbrown, C. (2013) *Understanding Schemas and Young Children*. London: Sage.

Athey, C. (2007) *Extending Thought in Young Children: A Parent–Teacher Partnership*, 2nd edn. London: Paul Chapman.

Athey, C. (2012) Beginning with the theory about schemas, in Mairs, K. and the Pen Green Team (ed. Arnold, C.) *Young Children Learning Through Schemas*. Oxford: Routledge.

Aubrey, C., David, T., Godfrey, R. and Thompson, L. (2000) *Early Childhood Educational Research Issues in Methodology and Ethics*. London: Routledge Falmer.

Bissex, G. (1980) *Gnys at Wrk: A Child Learns to Write and Read*. London: Harvard University Press.

Blaiklock, K. (2010) Assessment in New Zealand early childhood settings: a proposal to change from Learning Stories to Learning Notes. *Early Education*, 48(2), 5–10.

Blaxter, L., Hughes, C. and Tight, M. (1996) *How to Research*. Buckingham: Open University Press.

Bowlby, J. (1997) *Attachment and Loss, Volume 1*. London: Pimlico.

British Psychological Society (BPS) (2010) *Code of Human Research Ethics*. Leicester: BPS.

Brooker, L. (2002) *Starting School: Young Children Learning Cultures*. Buckingham: Open University Press.

Bruce, T. (1991) *Time to Play in Early Childhood Education*. London: Hodder & Stoughton.

Bruce, T. (2001) *Learning through play: Babies and Toddlers and the Foundation Years*. London: Hodder & Stoughton.

Bruce, T. (2004) *Developing Learning in Early Childhood*. London: Paul Chapman.

Bruce, T., Findlay, A., Read, J. and Scarborough, M. (1995) *Recurring Themes in Education*. London: Paul Chapman.

Caldwell, L. and Joyce, A. (eds) (2011) *Reading Winnicott*. London: Routledge.

Carr, M. and Lee, W. (2012) *Learning Stories: Constructing Learner Identities in Early Education*. London: Sage.

Carr, M., Smith, A.B., Duncan, J., Jones, C., Lee, W. and Marshall, K. (2009) *Learning in the Making: Disposition and Design in Early Education*. Rotterdam: Sense Publishers.

Christensen, P. and James, A. (eds) (2000) *Research with Children: Perspectives and Practices*. London: Falmer Press.

Claxton, G. (2002) *Building Learning Power*. Bristol: TLO.

Claxton, G. and Carr, M. (2004) A framework for teaching learning: the dynamics of disposition. *Early Years*, 24(1), March, 87–97.

Cousins, J. (1999) *Listening to Four Year Olds: How They Can Help Us Plan Their Education and Care*. London: National Early Years Network.

Da Ros-Voseles, D. and Fowler-Haughey, S. (2007) Why children's dispositions should matter to all teachers, beyond the journal. *Young Children on the Web*, September, 1–7. Available online at: www.naeyc.org (accessed 2 October 2014).

Dahlberg, G., Moss, P. and Pence, A. (1999) *Beyond Quality in Early Childhood Education and Care: Postmodern Perspectives*. London: Falmer Press.

Daniels, H. (2001) *Vygotsky and Pedagogy*. Oxford: Routledge.

Daniels, K. (2013) Supporting the development of positive dispositions and learner identities: an action research study into the impact and potential of developing photographic learning stories in the early years. *Education 3–13: International Journal of Primary, Elementary and Early Years Education*, 41(3), 300–315.

Das Gupta, P. (1994) Images of childhood and theories of development, in Oates, J. (ed.) *The Foundations of Child Development*. Milton Keynes: Open University.

David, T. (1998) (ed.) *Researching Early Childhood Education European Perspectives*. London: Paul Chapman.

De Lourdes Levy, M., Larcher, V. and Kurz, R. (2003) Informed consent/assent in children. Statement of the Ethics Working Group of the Confederation of European Specialists in Paediatrics. *European Journal of Pediatrics*, 162(9), September, 629–633.

Department for Education (2013) *Early Years Outcomes*. Crown Copyright.

Department for Education (2014) *Statutory Framework for the Early Years Foundation Stage*. Crown Copyright.

Donaldson, M. (1987) *Children's Minds*. London: Fontana Press.

Dweck, C.S. (2000) *Self-Theories: Their Role in Motivation, Personality, and Development*. East Sussex: Taylor & Francis.

Dweck, C.S. (2006) Mindsets: *How you can fulfil your potential*. New York: Random House.

Dweck, C.S. and Leggett, E.L. (1988) A social-cognitive approach to motivation and personality. *Psychological Review*, 95, 256–273.

Eng, H. (1931) *The Psychology of Children's Drawings*. London: Routledge & Kegan Paul.

Fernyhough, C. (2008) *The Baby in the Mirror: A Child's World from Birth to Three*. London: Granta Books.

Freire, P. (1996) *Pedagogy of the Oppressed*. London: Penguin.

Gerhardt, S. (2004) *Why Love Matters: How Affection Shapes a Baby's Brain*. Hove: Brunner-Routledge.

Goodman, Y.M. and Goodman, K.S. (1990) Vygotsky in a whole-language perspective, in Moll, L.C. (ed.) *Vygotsky and Education*. Cambridge: Cambridge University Press.

Graham, G. (2010) Behaviorism, in Zalta, E.N. (ed.) *The Stanford Encyclopedia of Philosophy*, Fall 2010 edn. Available online at: http://plato.stanford.edu/archives/fall2010/entries/behaviorism/.

Greig, A. and Taylor, J. (1999) *Doing Research with Children*. London: Sage.

Hall, B. (1998) *Madeleine's World: A Biography of a Three Year Old*. London: Secker & Warburg.

Hartley, R.E., Frank, L.K. and Goldenson, R.M. (1952) *Understanding Children's Play*. London: Routledge & Kegan Paul.

Hayward, K. (2012) Schemas and mark making, in Mairs, K. and the Pen Green Team (ed. Arnold, C.) *Young Children Learning Through Schemas*. Oxford: Routledge.

Hayward, K. and McKinnon, E. (2014) Making children's learning visible: uncovering the curriculum in the child, in McKinnon, E. (ed.) *Using Evidence for Advocacy and Resistance in Early Years Services*. Oxford: Routledge.

Holt, J. (1989) *Learning All the Time*. Ticknall: Education Now.

Isaacs, S. (1930) *Intellectual Growth in Young Children*. London: Routledge.

Isaacs, S. (1933) *Social Development in Young Children*. London: Routledge.

Johnson, H. (1928/72) *Children and the Nursery School*. New York: Agathon Press.

Kirkpatrick, E.M. (ed.) (1983) *Chambers 20th Century Dictionary*. Edinburgh: Chambers.

Laevers, F. (1993) Deep level learning. *European Early Childhood Research*, 1(1), 53–68.

Laevers, F. (1997) *A Process-Oriented Child Follow-up System for Young Children*. Leuven: Centre for Experiential Education.

Laevers, F. in collaboration with Daems, M., De Bruyckere, Declercq, B., Moons, J., Silkens, K., Snoecl, G. and Van Kessel, M. (ed.) (2005) *Well-being and Involvement in Care Settings. A Process-Oriented Self-Evaluation Instrument*. Leuven: Research Centre for Experiential Education. Available online at: www.kindengezin.be and www.cego.be.

Laevers, F. (2014) *The Journey to Excellence* (videos produced by Education Scotland). Available online at: www.journeytoexcellence.org.uk/videos.

MacNaughton, G. and Hughes, P. (2009) *Doing Action Research in Early Childhood Studies: A Step By Step Guide*. Maidenhead: Open University Press.

Mairs, K. and the Pen Green Team (2012) *Young Children Learning Through Schemas* (ed. Arnold, C.). Oxford: Routledge.

Matthews, J. (2003) *Drawing and Painting: Children and Visual Representation*, 2nd edn. London: Paul Chapman.

Miles, M.B. and Huberman, A.M. (1994) *Qualitative Data Analysis*, 2nd edn. London: Sage.

Ministry of Education (n.d.) Learning Dispositions. Available online at: www.educate.ece.govt.nz (accessed 1 October 2014).

Ministry of Education (1996) *Te Whariki: Early Childhood Curriculum*. Wellington, New Zealand: Learning Media Ltd.

Murray, J. (2011) Knock! Knock! Who's there? Gaining access to young children as researchers: a critical review. *Educate*, 11(1), 91–109.

Navarra, J.G. (1955) *The Development of Scientific Concepts in a Young Child: A Case Study*. New York: America Book-Stratford Press.

NCCA (2009) *Aistear: The Early Childhood Curriculum Framework*. Dublin: NCCA.

Nutbrown, C. (2012) A Tribute to Chris Athey. Conference talk at the Pen Green Centre, Corby, Northants.

Pahl, K. (1999) *Transformations: Children's Meaning Making in a Nursery*. Stoke-on-Trent: Trentham Books.

Pascal, C. and Bertram, A. (1997) *Effective Early Learning*. London: Hodder & Stoughton.

Piaget, J. (1951) *Play, Dreams and Imitation in Childhood*. London: William Heinemann Ltd.

Piaget, J. and Inhelder, B. (1973) *Memory and Intelligence*. London: Routledge and Kegon Paul.

Podmore, V.N. and Luff, P. (2012) *Observation: Origins and Approaches in Early Childhood*. Maidenhead: Open University Press.

Pollard, A. with Filer, A. (1996) *The Social World of Children's Learning*. London: Cassell.

Pratt, C. (1948) *I Learn from Children*. New York: Simon & Schuster.

Proulx, J. (2006) Constructivism: a re-equilibration and clarification of the concepts, and some potential implications for teaching and pedagogy. *Radical Pedagogy*, 8(1), Spring, 1–16.

Reid, S. (ed.) (1997) *Developments in Infant Observation: The Tavistock Model*. Hove: Routledge.

Rinaldi, C. (2006) *In Dialogue with Reggio Emilia*. Oxford: Routledge.

Roberts, H. (2000) Listening to children: and hearing them, in Christensen, P. and James, A. (eds) *Research with Children: Perspectives and Practices*. London: Falmer Press.

Roberts-Holmes, G. (2005) *Doing Your Early Years Research Project: A Step-By-Step Guide*. London: Paul Chapman.

Scott, J. (2000) Children as respondents: the challenge for quantitative methods, in Christensen, P. and James, A. (eds) *Research with Children: Perspectives and Practices*. London: Falmer Press.

Stern, D. (2003) *The Interpersonal World of the Infant*, 2nd edn. London: Karnac.

Sutton-Smith, B. (ed.) (1979) *Play and Learning*. New York: Gardner Press.

Sutton-Smith, B. (2009) *The Ambiguity of Play*. Cambridge, MA: Harvard University Press.

Tait, C. (2004) How children express their emotions and cope with their many daily transitions: 'chuffedness'. Paper presented at the EECERA Conference, Malta, September.

Tait, C. (2005) Chuffedness as an indicator of good quality in an infant and toddler nest. Paper presented at the EECERA Conference, Dublin, September.

Trevarthen, C. (2002) Learning in companionship. *Education in the North: The Journal of Scottish Education*, New Series, 10, 16–25.

Tulloch, S. (1993) *Reader's Digest Oxford Complete Wordfinder*. Oxford: Reader's Digest.

UN Convention on the Rights of the Child (1989) Available online at: www.unicef.org/crc/org/Rights_overview.pdf.

Von Glaserfeld, E. (1990) An exposition of constructivism: why some like it radical, in Davis, R.B., Maher, C. and Noddings, N. (eds) *Constructivist Views on the Teaching and Learning of Mathematics*. Reston, VA: NCTM, 19–29. Available online at: http://www.oikos.org/constructivism.htm.

Vygotsky, L.S. (1978) *Mind in Society: The Development of Higher Psychological Processes*. London: Harvard University Press.

Webb, L. (1975) *Making a Start on Child Study*. Oxford: Basil Blackwell.

Whalley, M. (2007) *Involving Parents in Their Children's Learning*, 2nd edn. London: Sage.

Winnicott, D.W. (1991) *Playing and Reality*. East Sussex: Brunner-Routledge.

Woodhead, M. and Faulkner, D. (2000) Subjects, objects or participants? Dilemmas of psychological research with children, in Christensen, P. and James, A. (eds) *Research with Children: Perspectives and Practices*. London: Falmer Press.

Index

Page numbers in *italics* refer to figures and tables.

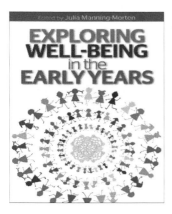

EXPLORING WELLBEING IN THE EARLY YEARS

Julia Manning-Morton

9780335246847 (Paperback)
October 2013

eBook also available

Children's experiences and well-being in their earliest years underpin and highly influence their future development and learning. Drawing on research with parents, children and a range of professionals in the early childhood field, this book considers how well-being is interpreted in the early childhood field. It includes snapshots of what our youngest children think about their well-being, and examines external environmental contexts that impact on well-being.

Key features:

- Focuses on appropriate pedagogical approaches and aspects of practice that support children's well-being
- Highlights the inseparability of adults' and children's well-being
- Prioritises children and families' socio-cultural contexts

www.openup.co.uk

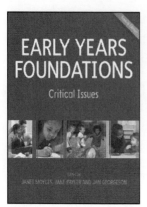

EARLY YEARS FOUNDATIONS
Critical Issues
Second Edition

Janet Moyles, Jane Payler & Jan Georgeson (Eds)

9780335262649 (Paperback)
February 2014

eBook also available

Among the many challenges facing early years professionals, there are continual dilemmas arising between perceptions of good practice, the practicalities of provision and meeting OfSTED requirements. This exciting and innovative new edition supports practitioners in thinking through their responsibilities in tackling some of the many challenges they encounter, for example, that children are still perceived as 'deficit' in some way and in need of 'being school ready' rather than as developing individuals who have a right to a childhood and appropriate early education.

Key features:

- Pedagogy
- Working with parents
- Difference and diversity

www.openup.co.uk

OPEN UNIVERSITY PRESS
McGraw - Hill Education

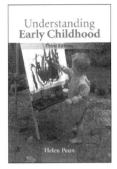

Understanding Early Childhood
3rd Edition

Helen Penn

ISBN: 978-0-335-26268-7 (Paperback)
eBook: 978-0-335-26269-4
2014

Understanding Early Childhood is a comprehensive textbook which offers broad and insightful perspectives across a range of themes on the ways in which we understand and study young children. Engaging and clear, it provides students with a user-friendly introduction to a number of difficult concepts and theories in early childhood education, drawing on research evidence from various countries and taking an interdisciplinary approach.

Key features include:

- A substantial and critically informed discussion of child development
- An updated overview of theoretical approaches and research methodologies
- Extended coverage of ethics

www.openup.co.uk

OPEN UNIVERSITY PRESS
McGraw - Hill Education

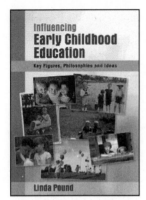

INFLUENCING EARLY CHILDHOOD EDUCATION
Key Figures, Philosophies and Ideas

Linda Pound

978-0-33524-156-9 (Paperback)
March 2011

eBook also available

Thinking about early childhood education will offer an academic and critical approach to the wealth of theories that underpin elements of current practice in early childhood care and education. It will focus on analyzing the rise and interconnectedness of theories of learning and development. It will range from key nineteenth century movements to progressive ideas of the twentieth century, encompassing psychoanalytic theories, deconstructing theories and constructivism and behaviourism.

Key Features of the text are:

- Different theories, ideas and philosophies linked
- Reflective questions at the end of each section designed to challenge different levels of thinking

www.openup.co.uk

OPEN UNIVERSITY PRESS
McGraw - Hill Education